NO MERCY,
NO JUSTICE

NO MERCY, NO JUSTICE

The Dominant Narrative of America
versus
the Counter-Narrative of Jesus' Parables

Brooks Harrington

FOREWORD BY *John C. Holbert*

CASCADE *Books* • Eugene, Oregon

For my father John,
who has taught me by his words and actions to be a person upon
whom people in trouble can rely.

For Maxine,
my love, conscience, and partner through everything for more than
forty years.

For our daughter Elizabeth and our son-in-law Gregg,
our daughter Katherine and our son-in-law Spencer,
our son Clay and our daughter-in-law Ashley,
and our grandchildren Lucas, Sarah, Livingston, and Harrison
—that they may walk God's way of justice and mercy.

For my coworkers in the vineyard of the Methodist Justice Ministry:
Juliana, Norma, Linda, Jodie, Yajaera, Nicole, and Sarah.

Table of Contents

Foreword

"NO MERCY, NO JUSTICE" is a very powerful book and not for the faint of heart.

Brooks Harrington is a unique Christian person. He was, and is, an attorney, having tried numerous cases, many of which had to do with abuse and domestic violence often against children. And he is an ordained clergyperson, now serving as the director of a justice ministry connected to First United Methodist Church in Ft. Worth, Texas. Let me say, by means of full disclosure, Brooks was a student of mine at Perkins School of Theology in a class of introductory preaching. He was a truly outstanding student and preacher then, topping his graduating class. But what was startling about him was his enormous commitment to the ideas he has expressed in this book, namely, the need to address with full honesty the deep and complex relationships between justice and mercy in the life of Christian faith. He speaks again and again of his work in the courtroom and on the streets among the homeless and abused of his city, probing for ways to address those two central issues in Christianity. He writes of the "dominant culture," the one we live in where justice is sought and applied often devoid of mercy. But also he addresses those Christians who would expect only mercy and never God's justice against their refusals to show mercy to all. In rich biblical analyses, from the prophets of Israel and especially from the potent parables of Jesus, he shows how justice without mercy may be calloused and cruel, while mercy without justice may be empty and simplistic.

I admit readily that the book was a real workout to read, not because the prose was not limpid and clear, but because I felt convicted again and again by my own complicity in the dominant narrative, and my own un-willingness to tender mercy to all and not to receive the justice from God that I should expect for my failings. I found the final chapter's retelling

Preface

IN THE STORIES TOLD about people, unless otherwise noted I have changed their names and a few identifying features to respect their privacy. The changed names are initially placed in quotation marks. The events retold in the stories are all true.

Introduction

TORAH, THE PROPHETS, AND the Gospels tell us that Jesus did not come just to open heaven for believers. Jesus did not come to be worshiped. Jesus did not come to sacrifice himself for us so that we needn't sacrifice ourselves for anyone. Jesus did not come to give and suffer for us so that we needn't give and suffer for anyone. Jesus did not come to found a church that would perpetuate itself by accumulating property and by keeping members comfortable and assured of God's love just the way we already are and just the way we already live. Jesus came to give birth and blueprint to a people who would together with Jesus' living spirit transform a world terribly broken. Jesus was sent by our Father to form and inspire a people who would build a community of justice and mercy that would challenge a world dominated by unjust and merciless competition for things, shallow pleasures, and the honor and power that comes with their accumulation. Jesus' life and teachings are the perfect incarnations of God's will for such a community. Faith and belief alone are not critical for the people of God. Love, manifested in our justice and our mercy, is critical.

Despite God's eternal will revealed in Torah, the prophets, and the Gospels, the world remains terribly out of whack. Millions of children, women, and men continue to suffer terribly from its injustice and mercilessness.

The community that Jesus came to form, and particularly the North American church, is failing in its God given mission. It seems most intent upon making "churchians," not Christians. Much of this is due to our own human nature. Our minds and souls are the battlegrounds between our urges to fear, fight and dominate, and our capacities for justice, mercy, and sacrifice for the common good. A cause of our failure is that we are seduced and overcome by a merciless and unjust account of

1

CHAPTER 1

Unjust and Merciless

ANYONE WHO DOESN'T RECOGNIZE that life is unjust and merciless is a fool. When I deny that life is unfair and merciless because I have received much more than my share of life's blessings, I am among the greatest of fools. That I might be personally so blessed does not make life itself any less unjust or merciless.

Life is unjust because of the random and merciless way that blessings and curses are meted out. Life is no less unjust and merciless because some are randomly born into plenty and hope and the promise of rescue from every crisis, while others are born into deprivation and despair and resignation. Some receive, as accidents of their births, intelligence and physical capacities valued in their cultures. Others are born with less valued intelligence and lesser physical capacities relative to their culture's ideals. Those who are blessed by their accidents of birth often turn from the call to empathy and assistance by blaming the less blessed and the unblessed for their plights. The abundantly blessed tell ourselves that the life that benefits us so much is not merciless and unjust because the less blessed and unblessed are responsible for their own deprivations. So we, the abundantly blessed, aided and abetted by the loudest voices in our culture, are practically indifferent to the suffering of the poor and their children.

I am afraid that I was a complete fool until one night in a ghetto in Washington, DC, when I hope I started being a little less of a fool. Joe Quantrille (his actual name) and I were out on the street at about 2 in the morning during the winter of 1980 or 1981, looking for a potential witness in a homicide case. Joe was a legendary homicide detective with the DC police department. I was an Assistant United States Attorney for the District of Columbia, assigned to the Career Criminal Unit. Because DC

What I visualize to this day about that night was how very dark it was outside the house, but how every light inside was burning, with so many black faces peering out of every window at us. The house was once a grand, single-family home from the days when that neighborhood was prosperous. The neighborhood had changed. This shooting and our response was happening in 1980 before the gentrification of that neighborhood, before the poor had been pushed out into Maryland. An enterprising slumlord had turned the house into a kind of apartment building, with a family unit of a man and a woman and some number of children living in each of the rooms.

When we entered the front door, we saw a staircase leading from the entry way to the second floor and the bottom of another staircase leading from the second to the third floor. A living room was to our left with a curtain between the entry way and that room. A man had pulled open the corner of the curtain, and was looking at us, with a child of maybe four holding onto his leg. We asked where the shooting was in the house, and how many men with guns were there. The man just pointed up the stairs and pulled the curtain shut.

Joe went up the stairs with his handgun drawn, with me right behind him. On the second floor, we saw a series of bedroom doors, all cracked opened with people peering out. From every room we could hear the sound of children crying and screaming. And we could smell the residue of gun smoke. Joe started going into the bedrooms, yelling "PO—lice!" slamming the doors open and leaping into the room, his handgun sweeping from side to side to cover the entire room. This caused the children in those rooms to scream harder. Angry men were cursing and yelling for him to get out. A woman said there was only one gunman and pointed to the bedroom at the end of the hall.

By then uniformed officers had responded. About six police including Quantrille were lined against the hallway walls, their pistols in hand. A sergeant wanted to get a SWAT team in but Joe ignored him, speaking firmly but calmly through the door, asking the gunman to give up and no one else would get hurt.

Abruptly, a beautiful, naked ten year old girl opened the door and stepped back. She was trembling as if she was cold, but the room seemed sweltering to me. In the room there was a man lying on his back on the bedroom floor with the top of his head blown off, a shotgun lying across his legs. The top of his skull was stuck in pieces to the wall behind him, blood and holes plastered around it. There was a woman lying on a bed

Through some of my thirty-five-plus years since that night, I have dreamed of those children. Strangely, I didn't dream or think about them at all for years after that night. Then they fought their way into my dreams. I have dreamed in particular of the three-year-old boy, always crying against that wall in that bedroom, unable to make a sound. And in some versions of this dream, that three year old takes me by the hand and leads me downstairs to the two, still sleeping toddlers on the mattress in the kitchen next to the blood. He doesn't say anything, and I still don't know what he wants me to do. Or I tell myself I don't know.

I don't know what became of these four children, but I can make an experienced guess. Maybe one of them turned out to be Superman or Wonder Woman and got out of that neighborhood without a criminal record, with his or her hope and possibilities tenaciously intact. But waiting for each of these three little boys and one little girl were lives of hopelessness and anger, drugs and violent crime, unemployment, illness, and multiple pregnancies with different unmarried partners. It is overwhelmingly likely that random, angry violence continued to be a routine in their "neighborhood." And the only response of the criminal-justice and predominant social systems was to assign a person like me, a prosecutor waiting at the end of the justice conveyor belt, insisting that they should be put in jail until they grew too old and tired to be angry and violent anymore.

During my year on the street investigating violent crimes in inner-city DC, the parts of the District where the tourists didn't go, the only hopeful and empowering voice I heard was the proclamation of Jesus' way by the African-American churches. I didn't know it at the time, but the experience in that house that night and the year in the ghettoes were my first steps toward this other Way. I hope that I am still walking toward it.

But why didn't I worry about those children at the time, when I could have gone back and found out their names and perhaps could have done something to help them? Maybe because the only version of justice and mercy I was hearing was the dominant system's. Under that system, those children were somebody else's problem until they committed felonies and got onto the conveyor belt to prison. Under that system, they certainly weren't due anything from me.

According to that system's notion of justice, what was "due" as a matter of justice to the homeless people in this story? Weren't they just the losers in the societal contest? Hadn't they just failed to compete

What mercy was due them within the dominant, secular system? Mercy that would really help, would really have made a difference? Doubtless you recognize a trick question. Because within the dominant system, mercy is never "due" to anyone from anyone, no matter their plight. Justice and mercy in this system are separate. Very little justice and no mercy are actually due.

But what about the justice and mercy due them within God's covenantal community under Jesus' counter-way? Why are we comfortable Christians so complacent about the plight of these children? Why do we professing Christians choose the dominant secular system's versions of justice and mercy, and not the counter-justice and counter-mercy of God and Jesus? Why do we aspiring Christians avoid seeing the lives of these children and the adults they grow up to be? And why do I adopt a terminology that makes Jesus' and God's way a "counter" narrative, and the dominant, secular narrative the baseline? God's Way should be the baseline, the standard against which all other ways are judged and compared. It is a testament to the effective dominance of the dominant, secular way that I use these sets of terms.

> He has told you, O mortal, what is good; and what does the
> LORD require of you, but to do justice, and to love mercy, and
> to walk humbly with your God.

At our discussion group after the service, our good friend Bill Lanford challenged me and everyone there to hear this passage anew. "How can God expect us to *do* justice while *loving* mercy? Aren't those contradictory? How are we to give people what they have coming as a matter of justice, while granting them what they don't have coming as a matter of mercy? Or is it the age-old dualism of making a distinction between how we ought to act and how we should feel? Doing hard but just things to people while wishing in our hearts that we could be merciful instead? And . . . just when does God ever succeed in doing both justice and mercy at once?" I recall thinking, "Wouldn't it be more like Jesus to 'do' mercy rather than justice? But don't we live in a world in which we desperately need both, yet a world in which we are required to choose one or the other?"

This issue of how to reconcile justice and mercy, of how to be just and merciful at once, of when and how to be just to one and when and how to be merciful to another, has been one I have been wrestling with through careers as an attorney and as an ordained United Methodist minister. The struggle is now focused in these two callings in my present ministry. In one career, I served as a prosecutor of violent crimes including rape and murder, and then Deputy Chief of Felony Trial as an Assistant United States Attorney in Washington, DC. Then I was a lawyer in private practice dedicated to winning civil lawsuits, protecting and vindicating my clients and acquiring wealth and comfort for myself and my family. In the other career, I was the pastor of an inner-city church in a neighborhood struggling with gang violence, drug addiction, teenage pregnancy, under-employment, poverty, hopelessness and all the rest I had seen in DC during my time there as a prosecutor. And for the last thirteen years and counting, I have been called to joint roles as lawyer and as clergy through a ministry founded at my church called the Methodist Justice Ministry. Through the Methodist Justice Ministry, two other attorneys, two legal assistants, and I provide free legal representation to obtain legal protections for indigent victims of family violence and child abuse and to provide financial and in-kind assistance, social work, free professional counseling, and pastoral support, advice, encouragement and friendship to enable woman and children to find new lives free of violence and fear.

The way our dominant secular, economic, and social system understands and pursues justice and mercy is neither just nor merciful. So the way that the people of God are called to understand and pursue God's mercy and justice has become a critical and personal issue for me in every way. In prayer and hope, I have turned to the way God understands and pursues justice and mercy, as attested by Scripture and particularly by the life and teachings of Jesus. The starting point for an aspiring Christian's understanding and pursuit is an understanding of *God's* justice and mercy and of how *God* pursues these.

> Thus says the LORD: "Do not let the wise boast in their wisdom, do not let the mighty boast in their might; do not let the wealthy boast in their wealth; but let those who boast boast in this, that they understand and know me, that I am the LORD; I act with mercy, justice and righteousness in the earth, for in these things I delight," says the LORD. (Jer 9:23–24)

God acts with justice *and* mercy . . . and in the earth. But how?

One set of related answers to this question, based upon the evidence, can be to deny that God has ever acted for justice and mercy "in the earth." God is either ineffective or distant and uninvolved, or effectively non-existent. Or justice and mercy are not important to God "in the earth" or anywhere, only right belief and praise. Or perhaps God's justice and mercy will only be acted out by God when each of us dies, or when the final and collective Last Judgment arrives. Under this last answer, God acts justly and mercifully "in the earth" only by keeping meticulous score of our justices and injustices, of our mercies and our mercilessness "in the earth," to be totaled up and acted upon "in the end."

Another set of answers includes that God acts mercifully to some and justly to others, but not mercifully and justly to both and everyone at once. Or God alternates justice and mercy, deciding when and to whom to be merciful or just based upon our deserving as judged by God. For instance, God is merciful to the victims of injustice and just to those who are merciless. Or God chooses who will be the beneficiaries of divine mercy capriciously or mysteriously. Based upon the assumption that God is always a mover behind all that befalls, the seeming randomness of life is strong evidence for this caprice or mystery. But a problem in this set of answers is that we humans, along with all of creation, desperately need a God who is just and merciful in ways that we can comprehend a little and try to follow and even imitate. Our dominant culture chooses to be

So in one of the earliest descriptions of God—God's self-description— God is described as merciful, giving what is not due, and as just, giving what is due.

In the Old Testament, God is described as "merciful" through derivatives of the Hebrew word *chesed*, also translated as "kindness," and through derivatives of the Hebrew *racham,* which is derived from the word for a woman's womb. And God is described as "just" with derivatives of the Hebrew *tsadeq* and *mishpat.* That Hebrew word *tsadeq,* like the Greek word *dikaios,* is variously translated as just and righteous.

> Gracious is the LORD and just. Our God is merciful. (Ps 116:5)

> Great is your mercy, O LORD; give me life according to your justice." (Ps 119:156)

> The LORD is just in all his ways, and merciful in all his doings. (Ps 145:17)

> Therefore the LORD waits to be gracious to you; therefore he will show mercy to you. For the LORD is a God of justice; blessed are all those who wait for him. (Isa 30:18)

Following these basic affirmations that God is just *and* merciful, the basic affirmation of the Torah is that a child of God must obey Torah to be just, and a critical part of that just obedience to Torah is mercifulness.

In Deut 10:17–20, the LORD gives Moses another self-description:

> For the LORD your God is God of gods and Lord of lords, the great God, mighty and awesome, who is not partial and takes no bribe, who executes justice for the orphan and the widow, and who loves the alien, providing them with food and clothing. You also shall love the alien, for you were aliens in the land of Egypt.

God's justice is fused with God's mercy to the vulnerable. So the people of God are likewise called to be just by being merciful to the vulnerable. "You shall not deprive a resident alien or an orphan of justice" (Deut 24:17). "Cursed be anyone who deprives the alien, the orphan and the widow of justice . . . All the people shall say 'Amen'" (Deut 27:19). Torah made mercy to the vulnerable a matter of the obligation of justice, not a matter of charity. (For further instance: Exod 22:25, 23:6, 23:11; Lev 19:9–10, 13, 33–34; 23:22, 25:1–55; and Deut 15:11, 24:12–15.)

The Hebrew prophets urge God's people to be just and merciful as well, in accordance with the justice and mercy of God, as in Micah 6:8:

CHAPTER 3

The Dominant Narrative of America

IF GOD IS INDEED committed to justice and mercy, if justice and mercy are inseparable aspects of God's Truth and Way, we Christians often show by the way we live our lives and spend our resources that we (God's so-called people) are not so committed.

Part of our failure is due to our fallible humanity. How hard it is for us to discern what is just and what is merciful in any given situation. How hard it is to overcome our fear and competitiveness with empathy and generosity, particularly when so many voices in our American culture are profiting from fear and advocating predatory competitiveness.

But very much of our failure to be just and merciful as God wills us to be is attributable to the power of the dominant, secular narrative of our time and place. This narrative has successfully shaped our characters and directed our behaviors. Even we aspiring Christians have accepted this dominant, secular view of justice and mercy provided by the culture, not God's justice and mercy revealed in Torah, the prophets, and particularly in the life and teachings of Jesus. This dominant narrative includes a version of justice and mercy that serves and supports the rest of the narrative.

Walter Brueggemann writes in the first chapter of his wonderful book *The Practice of Prophetic Imagination: Preaching an Emancipating Word*:

> [P]rophetic proclamation is the staging and performance of a contest between two narrative accounts of the world and an effort to show that the YHWH account of reality is more adequate and finally more reliable that the dominant narrative that is cast among us as though it were true and beyond critique.[1]

1. Walter Brueggemann, *The Practice of Prophetic Imagination: Preaching an Emancipating Word* (Minneapolis: Fortress, 2012), 3. Subsequent references will be made parenthetically.

do in fact live by more than one narrative. But the dominant narrative of our American culture seeks to dominate by condemning and belittling every other version of reality with its own standards about behavior, success, meaning and happiness. Our American dominant narrative is pervasive and relentless. Its proponents actively suppress any counter-narrative. The members of the dominant group associate economically and socially only with themselves. So any counter-narrative seems to these opinion makers and trendsetters to be odd and even ridiculous.

To me, it is useful to think about a dominant narrative as a song that plays everywhere and all the time to everyone. It is so loud, relentless, and pervasive that every other song sounds discordant and grating, and finally is not heard at all.

The narrative that seeks to be dominating, pervasive, and silencing of all other narratives in this American culture proclaims that success, honor, meaning, and happiness come solely from the maximum, continuing acquisition and consumption of expensive things and transient pleasures. The more expensive and ostentatious the things, the more honor and happiness to the consumer. The more transient and intense the pleasure, the more success and satisfaction to the consumer. We are conditioned to go from acquisition to acquisition, from pleasure to pleasure without ceasing.

Yet after we acquire the things and experience the pleasure, they prove not to fulfill the dominant narrative's promise. We are left still empty. And we cannot enjoy the moment. We are like children on Christmas morning who open present after present but enjoy none of them. When all the presents are unwrapped and scattered around the floor, we just want to unwrap more. So we move on in search of more stuff and more pleasure, hoping that these will finally fulfill the empty promise.

We are told by this narrative that in order for our lives to be happy and meaningful, we must have the most fashionable and trendy clothes, the most advanced and current electronics, the biggest house, the most expensive vehicle with the most bells and whistles, the memberships in the most exclusive clubs, the most expensive and self-indulgent vacations, the cruises in which we gorge ourselves on food and the trips to glitzy casinos where it is always time to drink and gamble, the most lavish "dining experiences," the most delicious and unhealthy foods, the beer or whiskey or wine of the insider, the beautiful, "most interesting" people, and the most casual sexual hook-ups with whomever we want

We should expect a certain amount of self-obsessed, other-destructive, and self-destructive behavior in any society, even those whose narratives teach that meaning and happiness come from sacrifice, attention to the common good, and care for the vulnerable and weak. But when self-obsessed, other-destructive, and self-destructive behavior becomes the standard, as it has in America, when such narcissistic behavior is celebrated, it is necessary to ask what about the society's particular narrative is inspiring this behavior. It is the height of hypocrisy for the proponents and main beneficiaries of our dominant narrative to blame its victims for its natural and necessary effects.

Within the culture of the dominant narrative, a problem or challenge suffered by an insider must be fixed or eliminated, and quickly, or we will be due to feel outraged at the injustice. If we consider something out of whack for ourselves or our family members, based upon our wants and fears, it must be put back in whack immediately and exactly how we want it. We insiders feel that we are due immediate elimination of whatever challenges us having what we want instantly. Our dominant narrative teaches this relentlessly. The narrative teaches us that *we* should not be kept on hold when we call our doctors for medication that will cure us immediately of all of our symptoms. The narrative teaches us that *our* child should be cured immediately of any illness. It teaches that *our* child should never be wait-listed instead of being admitted immediately to the preschool or private school or college of our choice. We should never be required to pay more taxes than we want or be denied some claimed deduction by someone we derisively call a "bureaucrat." We should never suffer delay in a loan being approved. No one should be driving slower than we are in the left highway lane, nor should anyone be tailgating us when we are driving in that lane. A plumber should respond immediately to our call about a leak in a water line in our wall. No one should ever tell us that we should not buy that gas-guzzling, club cab, pick-up truck, or that luxury Cadillac SUV, because of the effect upon the environment or the needs of the poor.

But within the culture of economically poor Anglo-Americans, African-Americans, and Hispanic-Americans, unwanted problems and even serious crises are often just to be endured because they will not be fixed. For the economically poor, the world is permanently out of whack. At first so many members of these communities feel that they are due better, but after a time they become resigned that they will not receive better.

Do not worry about your life, what you will eat or what you will drink, or about your body, what you will wear. Is not life more than food, and the body more than clothing? (Matt 6:25)

But the dominant narrative is so relentless, pervasive, and penetrating, and they are surrounded by so many peers whose focus is on the accumulation and personal enjoyment of more and more stuff and pleasure. At times they feel conflict within their own hearts and minds between the pervasive dominant narrative and the counter-word of Jesus. But regardless of the experience of spiritual conflict, the end result is that so many still spend a staggering amount of money on themselves and their families and a relative pittance on the poor, even though it may be a larger pittance than most all of their social and economic peers. I believe that the church has failed them by not insistently presenting them with the clear choice of God's counter-narrative that teaches that so much deeper, wider, and higher joy and satisfaction come from sacrificial generosity and mercy than from the self-obsessed acquisition of more stuff and more pleasure.

The American church itself lives by both of these conflicted narratives. Most churches have ministries to serve the poor, the outcast, and the vulnerable, true to the counter-narrative of the Christ. But these ministries are often moved away from the main church building so that the insider-members will not be made afraid by contact with the poor. And these same churches spend a relative pittance upon these ministries and relative fortunes upon the comfort of their members, the luxury of the church building, the quality of the organ and the music program, and the pleasure and intensity of the Sunday morning worship service. This all reflects the priority of stuff and pleasures of the dominant narrative. Too often, the church business officers, the property or foundation trustees, and the security staff have vetoed the church's proposed ministries to the poor and outcast. Many churches have locks and security guards to keep the poor, the outcast, and the vulnerable from even entering the main church property. And so many churches have clergy who are torn between discipleship within the counter-word of Jesus, and discipleship to the dominant narrative by maximizing their own salaries and material comforts. They well understand in their minds and souls that the church is to be the home of the living, counter-narrative of God. But the need to pay the increasing expenses on the growing church property and the desire to move up the clergy ladder based upon worship attendance and

and motion pictures that the greatest, most immediate pleasure in life is sex. What does she have to trade for stuff and pleasure?

In our Justice Ministry, we encounter daily young women who have turned to being valued by young men as sexual objects and who have turned to the immediate pleasure of uninhibited sexual gratification that is so glorified by the dominant narrative. In my experience, so many of these poor, young women—again of every race and ethnicity—feel that their sexuality is the only way to be somebody, to be noticed, to be wanted and valued and honored and loved, to obtain stuff and pleasure. So many of these poor young women are without any realistic hope that they ever will be able to better their material situations by delaying gratification. So they turn to the pleasure of casual sexual hook-ups now. To living with a series of men without waiting and testing whether their current man has any commitment to a true, lasting relationship or to parenting the child whom they helped conceive. To ornate tattoos as a source of individuality and distinction. To the escape of drug use. To running the streets while someone else cares for their children. To running up debt from predatory lenders so they can have the stuff they want now and feel the pleasure they think they need now. Particularly when confronted with the impact their choices have on their children, so many of these women have deep regrets, and the conflict in their hearts can be overwhelming. Part of each of them wants to be a good, nurturing, dependable mother. Part of them has heard the counter-narrative of love and sacrifice. But the dominant narrative of stuff and pleasure drowns it out, just as it does for the comfortable.

We have also encountered through the Ministry so many poor, young men who have experienced the same feelings and urges I describe for the young women. They have given up hope of distinguishing themselves, of being somebody, under the rules of the *agón* of the dominant narrative. Or they seek to be somebody under those rules through acquisition of stuff and intense but shallow pleasures of sex and drugs and the thrill of violence. They seek to prove their value by sexual conquests and then to avoid paying child support for the children they have fathered. They seek to prove their worth by violence against their peers and by drugs and crime, by a shallow masculinity that interprets physical intimidation of women and men as value and honor, and by the acquisition of gaudy cars and clothes with money they haven't made in honest employment. Yet I have seen these same young men display real shame and regret at their failure to support and parent their children. And I have had personal

CHAPTER 4

The Counter-Narrative of God

THE WORD OF GOD is always a narrative that is starkly counter to any used by dominant insiders to solidify their positons at the expense of the outsiders. As Dr. Brueggemann wrote in chapter 1 of his *The Practice of Prophetic Imagination: Preaching an Emancipating Word*, the people of YHWH are called to "a contestation between narratives." We are called to live into a counter-reality with counter-standards of meaning, honor, and satisfaction, counter-manners of behavior, and counter-goals, divisions, and boundaries. This has been true throughout the history of the counter-word of God.

For example, in the Moses story, the dominant narrative of Egypt was that the Pharaoh was himself the most powerful of gods, the current scion of an eternal, divine dynasty, due to be obeyed and served slavishly, so appropriately deaf to the cries of his suffering Israelite slaves. Pharaoh and all the Egyptians "set taskmasters over them to oppress them with forced labor" (Exod 1:11). "The Egyptians became ruthless in imposing tasks on the Israelites, and made their lives bitter with hard service in mortar and brick and in every kind of field labor. They were ruthless in all the tasks they imposed upon them" (Exod 1:13–14). The dominant narrative of the time was that the Hebrews were due to be enslaved at the Pharaoh's divine pleasure, Pharaoh was due to be served by the Hebrew slaves, their first-born sons were due to be killed, and these slaves were due to be required to make bricks without straw. Moses delivered a counter-narrative that YHWH, not Pharaoh, was the true, only, all-powerful God, and that YHWH, very unlike Pharaoh, heard and heeded the cries of the Hebrew slaves (Exod 2:23–24). The counter-narrative was that YHWH, not Pharaoh, was due to be worshipped and obeyed, and that YHWH, unlike Pharaoh, willed that the vulnerable be protected not

you become so impoverished that they sell themselves to you, you shall not make them serve as slaves. They shall remain with you as hired or bound laborers. They shall serve with you until the year of the jubilee. Then they and their children with them shall be free from your authority; they shall go back to their own family and return to their ancestral property. For they are my servants, whom I brought out of the land of Egypt; they shall not be sold as slaves are sold. You shall not rule over them with harshness, but shall fear your God. (Lev 25:35–43)

If there is among you anyone in need, a member of your community in any of your towns within the land that the LORD your God is giving you, do not be hard-hearted or tight-fisted towards your needy neighbor. You should rather open your hand, willingly lending enough to meet the need, whatever it may be. Be careful that you do not entertain a mean thought, thinking, "The seventh year, the year of remission, is near," and therefore view your needy neighbor with hostility and give nothing; your neighbor might cry to the LORD against you, and you would incur guilt. Give liberally and be ungrudging when you do so, for on this account the LORD your God will bless you in all your work and in all that you undertake. Since there will never cease to be some in need on the earth, I therefore command you, "Open your hand to the poor and needy neighbor in your land." (Deut 15:7–11)

If the person is poor, you shall not sleep in the garment given you as the pledge. You shall give the pledge back by sunset, so that your neighbor may sleep in the cloak and bless you; and it will be to your credit before the LORD your God. (Deut 24:12–14)

You shall not withhold the wages of poor and needy laborers, whether other Israelites or aliens who reside in your land in one of your towns. You shall pay them their wages daily before sunset, because they are poor and their livelihood depends on them; otherwise they might cry to the Lord against you, and you would incur guilt. (Deut 24:15)

You shall not deprive a resident alien or an orphan of justice; you shall not take a widow's garment in pledge. Remember that you were a slave in Egypt and the Lord your God redeemed you from there; therefore I command you to do this. When you reap your harvest in your field and forget a sheaf in the field, you shall not go back to get it; it shall be left for the alien, the orphan, and the widow, so that the Lord your God may bless you in all your

Thus says the LORD:
For three transgressions of Israel,
    and for four, I will not revoke the punishment;
because they sell the righteous for silver,
    and the needy for a pair of sandals—
they who trample the head of the poor into the dust of the earth,
    and push the afflicted out of the way;
father and son go in to the same girl,
    so that my holy name is profaned;
they lay themselves down beside every altar
    on garments taken in pledge;
and in the house of their God they drink
    wine bought with fines they imposed. (Amos 2:6–8)

Hear this word, you cows of Bashan
    who are on Mount Samaria,
who oppress the poor, who crush the needy,
    who say to their husbands, "Bring something to drink!"
The LORD God has sworn by his holiness:
    The time is surely coming upon you,
when they shall take you away with hooks,
    even the last of you with fishhooks. (Amos 4:1–2)

Whereas Amos spoke for the LORD to the insiders of the Northern Kingdom of Israel in the eight century BCE, Micah spoke to the privileged of the Southern Kingdom of Judah late in that same century. The dominant narrative of Judah was much the same as that of Israel. The landed wealthy and the royalty claimed blessing and sanction from the LORD to oppress the rural poor. They claimed that because they were blessed and beloved of God, they were invulnerable. Micah's counternarrative was:

And I said:
Listen, you heads of Jacob
    and rulers of the house of Israel!
Should you not know justice?—
    you who hate the good and love the evil, who tear the skin off my
    people,

I do not delight in the blood of bulls,
       or of lambs, or of goats.
When you come to appear before me,
       who asked this from your hand?
       Trample my courts no more;
bringing offerings is futile;
       incense is an abomination to me.
New moon and sabbath and calling of convocation—
       I cannot endure solemn assemblies with iniquity.
Your new moons and your appointed festivals
       my soul hates;
they have become a burden to me,
       I am weary of bearing them.
When you stretch out your hands,
       I will hide my eyes from you;
even though you make many prayers,
       I will not listen;
       your hands are full of blood.
Wash yourselves; make yourselves clean;
       remove the evil of your doings
       from before my eyes;
cease to do evil,
       learn to do good;
seek justice,
       rescue the oppressed,
defend the orphan,
       plead for the widow. (Isa 1:10–17)

How the faithful city
       has become a whore!
       She that was full of justice,
Righteousness lodged in her—
       but now murderers!
Your silver has become dross,
       your wine is mixed with water.
Your princes are rebels
       and companions of thieves.

Surely many houses shall be desolate,
> large and beautiful houses, without inhabitant.

For ten acres of vineyard shall yield but one bath,
> and a homer of seed shall yield a mere ephah.

Ah, you who rise early in the morning
> in pursuit of strong drink,

who linger in the evening
> to be inflamed by wine,

whose feasts consist of lyre and harp,
> tambourine and flute and wine,

but who do not regard the deeds of the LORD,
> or see the work of his hands!

Therefore my people go into exile without knowledge;
> their nobles are dying of hunger,

> and their multitude is parched with thirst. (Isa 5:7–13)

During the prophet Jeremiah's time, the dominant narrative of Judah was still that God's favor rested on the temple establishment. The LORD's glory was present in the temple. Israel was therefore due God's protection from any alien invader. Israel was impervious to any threat, regardless of whether the people observed Torah, because the LORD dwelled with them in the temple. The dominant narrative proclaimed that living as a child of God centered upon faithfully carrying out the temple ritual and obeying the dominant narrative of the priestly insiders. Jeremiah brought a counter-narrative:

> The word that came to Jeremiah from the LORD: Stand in the gate of the LORD's house, and proclaim there this word, and say, Hear the word of the LORD, all you people of Judah, you that enter these gates to worship the LORD. Thus says the LORD of hosts, the God of Israel: Amend your ways and your doings, and let me dwell with you in this place. Do not trust in these deceptive words: "This is the temple of the LORD, the temple of the LORD, the temple of the LORD."
>
> For if you truly amend your ways and your doings, if you truly act justly one with another, if you do not oppress the alien, the orphan, and the widow, or shed innocent blood in this place, and if you do not go after other gods to your own hurt, then I will dwell with you in this place, in the land that I gave of old to your ancestors forever and ever.

Blessed are you who weep now,

> for you will laugh.

Blessed are you when people hate you, when they exclude you and insult you and reject your name as evil, because of the Son of Man.

Rejoice in that day and leap for joy, because great is your reward in heaven. For that is how their ancestors treated the prophets.

But woe to you who are rich,

> for you have already received your comfort.

Woe to you who are well fed now,

> for you will go hungry.

Woe to you who are laughing now,

> for you will mourn and weep.

Woe to you when all speak well of you, for that is how their ancestors treated the false prophets.

(Luke 6:20–26)

In Paul's time, the dominant narrative proclaimed that the foundation of the power of the Roman Empire was the divinity of the Emperor. Temples raised to the "divine Augustus" proclaimed in stone in every provincial capital that Caesar was the "Son of God," and that he and his successors were "Lord," "Savior," and the bringers of "Peace" through military pacification. The dominant narrative proclaimed that it was therefore the will of God that Rome rule its vast empire with military might and tax its subject peoples. Paul bore God's counter-narrative that the Jesus crucified by Roman justice was resurrected by the only, true God and was the only, true "Son of God," the only, true "Lord" and the only true "Savior." God's counter-narrative proclaimed by Paul was that true power was found in weakness and sacrifice, and not in conquest and fear, and that true peace would come from love and not force of arms.

We would make a mistake if we believed that America has never been plagued by dominant narratives that have proven to be false. Narratives that seemed once so true and dominant in the history of America have been and are supplanted by narratives more approximating the counter-narrative of God. A once-dominant narrative relentlessly proclaimed that white males were willed by God to own black men, women, and children, steal their labor and oppress them as they wished without legal protections. A successor dominant narrative kept black men, women, and children in poverty and third-class citizenship through Jim Crow

CHAPTER 5

Justice and Mercy under the Dominant Narrative of America

WHAT ARE JUSTICE AND mercy? What makes an act "just" and what makes it "merciful"?

Generally, "justice" is rendering what is "due." For instance, the *Oxford English Dictionary* defines the "just" person as one who is disposed to "give everyone his or her due." The *Catechism of the Roman Catholic Church* states: "Justice is the moral virtue that consists in the constant and firm will *to give their due to . . . the neighbor.*"[1] And, "Society ensures social justice by providing the conditions that allow . . . individuals *to obtain their due.*"[2]

We also see this language describing justice as rendering what is "due" in passages of Scripture.

> You shall not pervert the justice due to the poor in their lawsuits. (Exod 23:6)

> Do not withhold good from those to whom it is due, when it is in your power to do so. (Prov 3:27)

> Ascribe to the Lord the glory due his name . . . (1 Chr 16:29)

> I will give to the LORD the thanks due to his righteousness,
>   and sing praise to the name of the LORD, the Most High. (Ps 7:17)

---

1. The *Catechism of the Roman Catholic Church* (New York: Doubleday, 1994), par. 1807, emphasis added.

2. Ibid., par. 1943, emphasis added.

What is due to me in a given situation from my friend, my co-worker, my supervisor, my employer? What is due to me from strangers I encounter when I am in need? What would be due to me as a matter of justice if I were the one lying on the side of the road, injured and unconscious?

Taking it further, is anything due from me to the creation? What is due the earth from our species? Anything at all? Is everything we are able to take from the sea, the sky, the earth, the rivers, and the ocean due to me and my species? As a matter of justice, is nothing due from us to the creation? Or is creation due for us to be protective stewards?

What is due to me from life? Nothing or everything I want? And if I do not receive from life ninety or more years of comfortable, protected, pain-free living, would I be justified in feeling that I am a victim of injustice, and that I have been cheated of my rights? Our basic outlooks on life are determined by what we feel is due and not due to us from life.

But what is life due from me?

What is due from me to God, and what is due to me from God?

Perhaps the most overlooked question is, what am I due from myself? What pangs of my conscience or urges from my appetites and fears should I observe, indulge, or deny? What permissions am I due to be given from myself? What limitations and self-imposed disciplines am I due to have imposed upon me by myself? What times of quiet and meditation, or of hedonistic pursuits? What endurance of hardships or flight from burdens? What sacrifices and what selfishness? What living for others and what living for myself? What impulsiveness and what prudence am I due to be granted by myself? What formation of character and what giving in to temptation? Am I due from myself to choose to be merciful or just? Or am I due from myself only to seek my own wealth and pleasure? Have you known individuals who have been unjust to themselves? Have you never been unjust to yourself by failing to render to yourself what was due? All these issues about justice to myself beg the questions of who and what I am and therefore what that "I" is due from me. Am I just my appetite for food, sex, and pleasure? Or am I primarily my mercy and justice?

From beginning to end, Holy Scripture is mainly about three justice issues. What is God due from me? What is the other person due from me? What am I due from myself?

Consider then the general definition of "mercy." Our English word "mercy" is taken from the Old French *merci,* which meant pity. According to the *Merriam-Webster Dictionary,* "mercy" means "kind or forgiving

To be too merciful—to give people too much too often of what they are not due—undermines the justice and integrity of the competition. More than occasional mercy would make people less self-reliant, would undermine their work ethic, and would reduce the productivity and efficiency of this system. The dominant narrative teaches that rendering only what people are due is critical to achieving excellence. Softening this dominant view of justice that people are due whatever they can win, but not due what they do not win, would undermine the system. Within this narrative, human beings are only motivated to work hard by selfishness and greed for things and personal pleasure, not by the common good or by the needs of the suffering and vulnerable. If you change the system so that people are provided what they have not killed for themselves, "these" people will not be motivated to work hard. You will be rewarding failure, which is definitely not just.

But in truth the starting lines of the competition for stuff and pleasure are segregated, with one set of competitors up front and with many, many more competitors starting miles behind or not even allowed onto the same track in the same stadium. The reality of our society is that the same goal is not possible for all competitors, even as the narrative says that only those who reach that one goal will be successful and happy. The children of the outsiders don't get to run for the same finish line as the children of the insiders, and they can't start from the same starting blocks. The dominant narrative conditions us to believe that this is just, as if this injustice and mercilessness to the children of the outsiders is all that is due them.

Within the world created by the dominant narrative, we are not to live as if our fellow citizens were neighbors. We on the inside live as if our society is a *Gran Prix*, a race among elite competitors for the grand prize of ostentatious wealth, shallow pleasures, and honor based upon acquisition of that wealth and pleasure. The rest, and definitely the clients of the Methodist Justice Ministry, live out the *Hunger Games*, not only for food and necessities, but for the stuff, shallow pleasures, and so-called honor that will not satisfy. As the prophet wrote: "Why do you spend your money for that which is not bread, and your labor for that which does not satisfy?" (Isa 55:2).

Somehow, claims the narrative, if I focus only on my rights and prerogatives, my appetites, urges, desires and so-called needs, an invisible hand will ensure that the entire system and everyone in it will benefit. So I receive from the narrative not just license but also encouragement to be

occasional charitable contributions. I am speaking about sacrificial mercy acted out from an individual's heart to another individual. How many
people do you know, love, and admire who go years without personally
helping someone in need who isn't a member of their immediate family
or close social circle? This has not always been the way in this country.
Neighbors helped one another, sacrificed for one another, helped get one
another through hard times. My experience in the last thirteen years
working in the Methodist Justice Ministry, going into our clients' homes
and witnessing their regular, sacrificial generosity, is that the economically poor commonly help others outside their immediate family. It's the
comfortable—the winners of the *agón*—who generally do not. This is the
effect of the dominant narrative.

The great lie of the dominant narrative is that anyone within our
system can by hard work acquire the things and pleasures necessary for
success, honor, and satisfaction. I have known hundreds and hundreds
of men and women who work themselves to physical and emotional exhaustion at multiple jobs that don't pay enough to support a family, to
save, or to get out of debt. They have to turn to predatory pay-day and
title lenders to make it through any crisis, and the burden of those debts
then bury them deeper into the grave of poverty. The place they start on
the material ladder has nothing to do with their merit and everything to
do with accidents of birth. The place they are stuck on that ladder has
nothing to do with a lack of hard work. I know children of the rich and
accomplished who just can't seem to find hoe handles to fit their hands.
But they inherit their parents' positions on the ladder. I know personally
hundreds of young people from poor families who have no help, no soft
landing spot, absolutely no room for mistake, and so no grace. I know
hundreds of young people from rich families—inheritors of the winners of the *agón*—whose every transgression is excused, covered up, and
forgotten. Surely there are the amazing exceptions—the young person
from a terrible home circumstance who has extraordinary gifts and finds
mentors and sponsors along the way to enable them to "rise above their
raising." These special, admirable individuals are used by the dominant
narrative to serve as justification for a merciless system.

But the claim that anyone can make his or her way out of poverty today with hard work is a terrible lie. I can tell you anecdotally that people
in America in low-paying jobs will never get out of poverty, no matter
how hard they work. There is no direct connection between wealth and

The dominant narrative appeals to and is the product of the worst aspects of our beings—fear, suspicion, greed, the will to dominate, and the resulting mercilessness. As we shall see, the counter-narrative of God and Jesus appeals to and is the product of the image of God within each of us—humility, self-discipline, empathy, generosity, a yearning for true community, and the resulting mercifulness.

murders and rape cases. (Felony II cases were all the rest of the felonies, from murder in the second degree to simple drug possession and theft.) A Felony I assignment was the goal of almost every prosecutor in that office. I had succeeded. With that attainment and experience behind me, I was on my way to an eventual position in a large and prestigious DC law firm, to an apex position in the system created by the dominant narrative.

But then there was "Karen," I will call her. One of my very first Felony I cases. The main challenges in this prosecution were to qualify Karen as mentally competent to testify and then to persuade and enable her to do so. There was no witness to this crime besides Karen. The assailant had used a condom, and so there was no semen to find and test. There were signs of trauma, but this man had not been caught in the act, and Karen was scared and didn't report what happened until late the next morning. There was a party downstairs in her mother's home and every man there had gone upstairs to use the bathroom. Karen really needed to testify for me to obtain a conviction. She knew the assailant after many encounters and her identification of him by name and photo was likely to be sufficient for conviction, *if* she was able to testify before a judge and jury.

Karen was not merely thirteen and intellectually impaired. She suffered from club foot, dwarfism, a deformed hip, and hydrocephalus. She had an almost bare skull, with a few wisps of hair growing out the top of her forehead, and a normal sized trunk for her age. But she had shriveled little legs and no use of one hand. She couldn't walk or even crawl. And she possessed the biggest, toothiest, face crinkling smile that makes tears well up in my eyes even now, thinking about her as I am typing this.

Karen had a devoted mother and three loving siblings. The mother could not afford in-home nursing assistance for Karen, so had to quit her low-paying job to care for her. The family's only income, as I recall it now, was from Social Security disability for Karen, food stamps and rent assistance. Maybe Aid to Families with Dependent Children was still in place back then. Regardless, that family was barely getting by, going from financial crisis to financial crisis. But there was an abundance of love in that home.

Karen had to testify or this man might get away scot-free to do it again. Both Karen and her assailant were due the justice of his being convicted and sentenced to jail for as long a sentence as I could obtain for him.

The court appointed defense attorney did his duty and challenged Karen's competence to testify. Competence for a witness in this setting

fantasy, able to recount a history and understand and answer questions and competent to testify.

But that left the challenge of getting Karen to tell her terrible, embarrassing story, complete with the legally required anatomical details, in front of Chief Judge Moultrie and then in a courtroom full of absolute strangers, by far the largest group of people she had ever spoken before. If she was too shy or scared to testify, she was indeed incompetent. This was to be a functional test. I would be very limited in how much I could ask her leading questions. But if she could not tell her story, there would be no evidence before the jury, and Chief Judge Moultrie would have to dismiss the case.

So I went repeatedly to Karen's mother's house so Karen would know and trust me. Looking back on it, it was a privilege to be welcomed so warmly and trustingly into that home.

Karen did well in the initial hearing before Chief Judge Moultrie, and he ruled that the jury could hear her account. And when the trial came, and after the jury had been picked, after our psychologist had testified, and Karen's mother had told the jury all about Karen and her disabilities and her courage and her hidden but actual intelligence, and after the circumstantial evidence had been offered, I wheeled Karen into the center of that circular courtroom, her tiny body swallowed by the chair, looking nervously from side to side until she saw the man who raped her. As I am typing this, I have tried 136 cases to jury verdict in my career, and I remember it as the most dramatic moment in my entire courtroom career. The Chief Judge let me sit in a chair right in front of Karen in the middle of the circular court well, so she was essentially telling her new, good friend the story, including the legally necessary anatomy. When I asked her if she could identify the man who did this to her, she pointed right at him, and called him by name. To lessen the inherent prejudice of the in-court identification process when a victim or witness points at the only person sitting at the defendant's table next to the defense attorney, the Chief Judge had positioned the defendant in a seat in the gallery among other African-American men. Karen had no hesitation in identifying him.

Some of the jurors were crying so hard after her testimony that Chief Judge recessed us for the day, before defense counsel cross examined Karen. And there were two male jurors who looked as if they wanted to come out of that jury box and jump the defendant. So we got them out of there for the evening.

At first I refused without hesitation. I still hated the rapist. The longer this very good defense attorney spoke, the angrier I felt. Because I knew he was right. I gave the excuse that I couldn't be intervening in every case of a prisoner in danger in Lorton. The prison officials have to run that place. The violence in that place was a deterrent against people committing crime. I was sure (I wasn't) that he was overstating the risk to this particular defendant, I said.

But in my heart, his murder by a fellow inmate would feel like justice truly and finally rendered, what this horror of a human was merely "due." I thought he was "due" whatever he got at the hands of his inmates. That was that. Justice had been delayed, but wasn't going to be denied much longer.

I went home that evening. I couldn't sleep. I was thrashing around the bed so much that my wife Maxine asked me what was wrong. She wouldn't let it go. I finally told her. She recalled Karen's case very well, of course. We had lived that together. My wife listened and finally told me that she was afraid that if the defendant was killed, I would come to regret not having acted to prevent it. No, she agreed, he was definitely due much worse than he had received. But not even our justice system provided for the death penalty, much less a suffering death. And my failure to do what I could would be doing an injustice to myself, something that I was not due. I was better than that, she said. And she had noticed that the job was turning me meaner than I had to be. It alarmed her. Do it for me, she said. Not for him.

So, mainly for myself and my wife, I made the call. I recommended that he be moved. And he was. I have no idea how much weight my request carried. But I made the request.

Despite my hatred, I felt better after I had done that. In retrospect, it may have been the effect of the gospel I had heard from those African-American churches.

Under the dominant narrative's version of justice, I should have let him die. He certainly wasn't "due" the mercy he wanted—to be moved and saved, at least for a time. He was due worse than he had received. But I wasn't due making myself a killer.

I don't know where the defendant is now. This was about thirty-five years ago. He may have died in prison. It's likely that the parole board denied parole every time he came up, or he became institutionalized and didn't want out.

to her. Respect, friendship, attention, presence, love, material help, laughter, and tears.

**

As an Assistant United States Attorney and eventually Deputy Chief of Felony Trial, in the name of "justice," I was instrumental in sending hundreds of young, impoverished, violent men to prison for the rest of their youths and into their middle age. I personally tried eight first-degree murder cases to jury verdict. The one case I recall best is the one where a merciless injustice was done at my hands. In that case, I obtained the wrongful conviction of a stone-cold innocent man for first-degree murder and rape, only to have him totally exonerated of the crimes by incontrovertible DNA evidence after he had served twenty-eight years in prison. I was convinced at the time I tried the case that I was righteously meting out justice to the defendant and protecting the community from a predator. I was convinced then that if he were not convicted, he would walk out of the courtroom and murder and rape again. I was tragically wrong. In fact, I was inflicting a merciless injustice. In retrospect, I didn't "do justice" or "love mercy" in that case. My failure has haunted me since I found out what I did. It has been no consolation to either me or my innocent defendant that I was "just doing my best with the evidence that I was told I had." Without my conviction that the defendant was guilty, without my talent, and without my commitment to winning the competition of the trial, this merciless injustice would never have happened. Such, I fear, is not so atypical of the human justice system.

Briefly stated, the facts of the case are these. In 1981, a female student at a local university was working late at a business in a building close to Rock Creek. She left work close to midnight and tried to walk home to her apartment. She never made it. A search party from her work went out the next morning and found her body in thick brush on the banks of Rock Creek, maybe a hundred yards from the building. She had been raped and shot in the head. The district and particularly students at the university were in an uproar, of course. I think it was fair to say that the police were under intense pressure to identify the murderer and lock him up.

The facts of this investigation and prosecution have been widely publicized after the exoneration. They have been the subject of a civil suit

Regardless, all of the prosecutors who handled the case through the grand jury investigation were convinced the defendant did the crime, and we were afraid of the consequence to the community if he was acquitted. I was convinced the defendant committed the crime. The so-called microscopic match between the defendant's pubic hair and the hair recovered from the rape and murder victim's body corroborated the snitch's claim that the defendant confessed the crime to him.

There are two terrible mistakes that the criminal-justice system can make. One is that an innocent man is convicted. The second is that a guilty man is acquitted. In retrospect, given that I now know the defendant was stone-cold innocent, I am afraid that I was too concerned about the second type of mistake.

Almost three decades later, when I was the legal director of the Methodist Justice Ministry, I received a call from my old office, informing me that DNA evidence had exonerated the defendant. The snitch must have lied. But that still left the hair match about which the FBI hair examiner had been so positive and aggressive at trial. Then I was told that the "science" of hair comparison, and the significance of so-called "microscopically indistinguishable" hair comparisons, had been discredited after the conviction but before the exoneration.

Comparisons of DNA from the developing national collection bank had revealed that the rapist and murderer of the victim was actually a man who worked as a janitor in the business where the young murder victim had been working before she tried to walk home.

An innocent man had served twenty-eight years in prison for a crime he did not commit. Twenty-eight years without seeing or holding a baby, or hearing a child laugh, or touching a woman, or petting a dog, or walking through a flowered field, or sitting at a café and watching lovers walk by, or drinking a beer. Twenty-eight years in fear, stoking his own anger and resentment.

We have all read about the numbers of exonerations produced by DNA, after innocent people spent years in prison for crimes they did not commit. We have all read about prosecutor's offices resisting exonerations, dragging their feet. And I fear there is a lack of concern and compassion by many of our fellow citizens for prison conditions, and for the plight of people on parole, and even for people wrongly convicted. "So what if we convict an innocent person occasionally. I'm sure that person committed crimes for which he was never charged." Why are we so sure? Because they are black or brown or poor? And why do we think

their lives. They were no longer "them" to me, to be feared, suspected, and shunned like stray dogs. "They" had become "him" and "her," Romero and Claude and Mary Beth and Maria. I learned some things. The majority of the homeless are employed. They just don't make enough to get into their own apartment. Maybe half have criminal records, which, like my innocent defendant, disqualifies them from public housing. This culture never forgets and forgives when it comes to a felony, no matter how long ago it was committed, no matter how young the person was when they made the mistake. And maybe half are homeless because of disability or disease, or addictions that could be treated if they had resources. Many people I met on the street, in the homeless shelters and in the homeless camps, had been one illness or one accident away from losing their job and being evicted. When that accident or illness came, they became homeless. When their particular disaster occurred, they had no place to go but to a homeless shelter or camp. And the longer they stayed homeless, the less likely they would ever be able to get free of it.

One of the worst prejudices in the United States is the pre-judging that whatever homeless person you encounter is lazy, a liar, a thief, and a danger. So every homeless person is to be shunned, and barriers are to be built to keep them out. One of the worst consequences of homelessness is that people will not look you in the face. The churches are among the worst at giving in to prejudice and fear about the homeless being in the same facilities where their members are. Churches that provide a ministry to the homeless will typically build or use another facility a distance away from the main church building, and hire security to keep all homeless persons out of the main church. What justice and mercy are they following? God's or the dominant narrative's?

I received the greatest of mercies from my innocent defendant, one I definitely was not "due" as a matter of justice. When I was told he was innocent, I was advised to say nothing publicly because a lawsuit was in the offing against the District and the investigating police officers. I was asked to say nothing that would embarrass my old prosecutor's office. Candor and apology were to be avoided within the dominant narrative. Certainly, I should not admit making any mistake myself. Dozens of people, no doubt out of kindness to me, told me that I had nothing to regret or apologize for. There had been no DNA back then. I was "just doing my job with the evidence I had."

It didn't feel that way to me. I was an aspiring Christian and an ordained minister of the United Methodist Church. So I wrote my innocent

group health-insurance coverage policies that had the effect of excluding coverage for a birth defect of an already covered family's newborn. Their contractual coverage of the newborn would not start until the second day of an infant's life, and would not cover "pre-existing conditions," meaning conditions with which the child was born. Since, by definition, a "birth" defect is present at birth, and since the coverage didn't start until the child had turned two day's old, a birth defect was a "pre-existing condition" that went uncovered. Any care that was needed to treat that birth condition was not covered by the policy.

Imagine being a working person with health-insurance coverage through your work. Imagine being pregnant and being assured that your insurance covered the costs of your prenatal care, your labor and your delivery, and any complications you suffer. Imagine being assured that your coverage would pay for care for your newborn, just as it pays for medical care for any member of your family. The blessed day comes, and your child is born. But you learn immediately that this child has a serious birth defect and is in critical need of immediate treatment. Your little girl was born without fully formed joints in two of her limbs. Unless she started immediately with expensive surgery and then therapy, to cut and loosen the connective tissue and create joints halfway down her limbs, your little girl would never be able to use those limbs normally.

But then you are informed that your group health-insurance policy does not cover treatment for this condition because it is a birth defect, a condition pre-existing the start of the child's coverage on day two of her life. The needed treatment will costs hundreds of thousands of dollars, but you don't have the money and don't have the credit rating or collateral assets to get it. You make a little too much income to qualify for any government assistance but not nearly enough income to pay for the care yourself or secure the loan. The small window of time in which your little girl's condition can be treated effectively passes. Now her condition is permanent. Your beautiful little girl, and she is beautiful, now has sticks for limbs.

The insurance company saved millions and millions of dollars by this standard one-day delay in beginning coverage for newborns, using this standard exclusion of coverage for "pre-existing" birth defects. Families lost those same millions. Some borrowed to pay for the needed treatment and went into bankruptcy when they couldn't pay off their debts. More often, the child just failed to receive the needed treatment. The human toll to the families hit by this was enormous.

ask for—reimbursement of their actual, out-of-pocket expenses to treat the condition—without punitive damages. It wasn't the company's fault that this family failed in its duty to obtain that treatment or that the parents were uninformed consumers. The claims adjusters were guilty of no more ignorance of the new law than the parents were. Wasn't it up to the family to call it to the attention of the adjuster? What the company had made was merely a business mistake that violated one small law of the state insurance code. At most, it was merely an illegal business decision; it wasn't an unjust or outrageous one.

Underlying that argument, and the conduct of this company, was the same version of justice, of what is due to whom from whom, of the dominant narrative. It was up to that poor family to win the *agón* with the insurance company, to "get" the coverage, to kill the coverage so they could eat it. Since the family had failed to force the company to provide it, they didn't win the competition. So they weren't due the coverage. It was an argument remarkable for its candor.

For the company executives, what they claimed was "due" to this family was completely divorced from mercy, from the human toll of what they were claiming. To them, this suffering family, with this little girl, weren't neighbors, weren't members of the same community. They were competitors trying to win some of the company's money. I feel certain that many of these executives were nominal Christians. Some, at the least, likely attended church on Easter and Christmas. Many may have worshipped faithfully, tithed, and considered themselves devout "Bible believers." But I cannot discern how their beliefs and the teachings of Torah and the prophets and Jesus impacted the cold, detached, unjust, and merciless way they treated this and so many families.

A large part of it was the dominant narrative and its version of justice and mercy. Good people entered the corporate board room, the belly of the dominant narrative, and removed their faith like it was a dirty shirt. They were probably kind and supportive to one another, caring and considerate of the secretaries and administrators who worked for them, gentle to their spouses and children and elderly parents. But professionally, they were predators. And the feeling they surely had deep in their souls where the image of God dwelled, that what they were doing was unjust and merciless and just plain wrong, was killed by the dominant narrative. But I still wonder, while they were carrying out this scheme to save the company money and maintain profits for the shareholders, did

damages. To me, the jury essentially found the company guilty for obeying the teachings of the dominant narrative. Within the world created by the dominant narrative, that little girl was due only what she could take from that company. The rules of the corporate competition dictated that the executives in that company maximize the profits and minimize the loses. That rule of corporate competition, produced by the dominant narrative, trumped the statute. Honoring that family's claim would have been a loss.

Justice? Did that beautiful little girl receive what she was due? Well, from whom? And when? I'm certain that that little girl, grown now into a woman, would trade all that money for the ability to be able to play with her own children like a normal mom.

As this suit was ongoing, insurance companies were lobbying Congress to eliminate such bad-faith lawsuits against health-insurance companies in state courts, to force claimants into arbitration and to free insurance companies from the justice meted out by outraged jurors. In other words, they sought to change the rules of the game this one company hadn't followed in this case anyway.

**

After one semester in seminary, I was appointed to a dying United Methodist church in one of the poorest neighborhoods of my city.

Two of the first people I met there I'll call "Lupe" and "Sonia." Lupe was an eight year old girl. Her mother was in prison on a long sentence for drugs. I don't think Lupe knew who her father was, but I may recall that incorrectly. In any event, he wasn't in her life and he didn't contribute anything for her. Lupe was raised by her maternal grandfather. I'll call him "Bert." They lived about a quarter mile from my church, on the other side of a busy four-lane street lined with bars and pay-day loan shops and immigration *abogados* and *notarios*. Bert and Lupe lived on a dead-end road that wasn't paved, that wasn't even graveled, and that became impassable when it rained. Not many city councilpersons ever drove down that street. The house that Lupe and her "Grandad" lived in had holes where many of the window frames should have been. There was junk scattered in the front and back yards. Rats lived in the junk. There wasn't much distinction between the inside and the outside of the house, in terms of clutter or temperature, although it was a little dryer

four-lane, city street. And Bert didn't have a phone. His truck was chronically broken down. Plus, the school was uphill from his house, and he had a serious breathing issue. So Lupe would be quarantined all alone in a lice room at the school until it was time to go home. Then she would be told not to return until Bert had eliminated the lice with a lice shampoo and by picking out all of the lice nits one by one from her hair.

The other children made fun of Lupe mercilessly. Her clothes were always dirty and rumpled, her hair was matted and unwashed, her socks never matched. She was short and overweight. And she had lice. They shunned her company, even on the playground. Yet Lupe was so sweet and desperate for friendship and affection. It was heartbreaking.

I talked to Bert about the lice. He immediately got angry. He couldn't afford "the goddamn shampoo." He didn't have the time or the eyesight or the lighting (or the sobriety) to pick all the nits out. He was sure that Lupe wasn't getting the lice from his house. It must be from the other kids at that school.

"Well, Bert, if you aren't using the shampoo and picking out the nits one by one, what are you doing?"

He said he was spraying WD–40 on her pillow.

I'm not making up a syllable of this.

I obtained a signed paper from Bert allowing me to take Lupe from the school to my church to shampoo her hair and pick out the nits. Whenever she had lice, the school was to call me about it, not Bert. We purchased a supply of lice-killing shampoo, some tweezers and a bright flashlight. A woman church member would always come to the church to help when I called. It was a weekly battle. Lupe was so grateful.

Yet there were greater concerns about Lupe's living situation. Bert's residence was something of a gathering place for men of like lifestyle. They were all drunk most of the time I went by. One consolation was that there didn't seem to me to be any hard-drug use. Some of these men were not old. Lupe was very vulnerable. And she was guileless.

One woman of the church took Lupe under her wing. Her name was "Virginia." If it had been up to Virginia, she would have adopted Lupe. Lupe was spending many nights at Virginia's home, which was modest but very clean and a palace compared to Bert's place. It was a palace of welcome and love by any standard. Lupe was begging Bert to let her stay overnight with Virginia more and more. And Virginia was trying to teach Lupe how to be a young lady, including what to avoid and when to make an outcry.

to a house only four blocks away from my church. It was a single story, clapboard residence with a tall, wrought-iron fence around it, the only fence like that in the neighborhood. The gate was chained with a padlock. The girl and boy started to get out.

"Wait. Tell me first what we are doing here."

The girl said that the house was owned by an old man who manufactured and sold methamphetamine there. And he exchanged meth for sex with women like their mother. They had found their mom there in the past. The children told me this in a matter-of-fact manner. Of course they knew about such things. What thirteen- and six-year-old children do not?

"You think we can just walk through that gate? It looks locked to me."

"He'll let me in," said the girl.

"Why?"

"Because he wants to f*** me." She was thirteen years old.

"That's why you brought me along, to protect you?"

"No, we brought you along because you're a lawyer."

"What good is that?"

"You can threaten to have him locked up if he doesn't let her go?"

I passed over her mistake about what my kind of lawyer can do.

"Why do you think she is in there?"

"We were here before, and he wouldn't tell us whether she was or wasn't. He's never refused to tell us before. So we think she is there. Or she has been."

"You've been through this with your mom and this old man before?"

"Yes."

All three of us walked to the gate, and the girl leaned on the buzzer. Eventually, we could see a light in a window where a curtain parted. Then the front door opened in, behind a barred outer door.

"Who's that with you?" called an old man's voice.

"My lawyer," called the girl.

"Sir, I am just the pastor of the Methodist church a few blocks from here. These children came to me because they are worried that their mother is in your house. She hasn't been home for a while. Can you tell them whether she is in there?"

"So you ain't a lawyer?"

"I am a lawyer. But I am here as a pastor to help these children."

of them. The girl directed me to turn off my lights and to drive behind the office shack and stop. Then she got out of my car and crept up beside one of the shacks, peering in a side window. She came running back to the car.

"She's in there! She's lying on the bed. I don't see no one else in there."

The little boy jumped out of the back seat. He ran up to the door to the motel room and began pounding on it. "Momma, Momma! Open up! It's me! Come home, momma! Please come home! Please!"

This went on for some minutes with no response. A light came on in the motel office and the rooms all around. The girl went back to the side window and tried to pull open the screen and window and crawl in. Just then, the motel room door jerked open.

"I'm coming, dammit. You don't have to wake the dead."

It seemed like we just had.

During the years to come, I really got to know Sonia. Bert was her father. She had a brother and a sister, both of whom were in prison for drugs. Sonia was the oldest sibling. Her mother was diagnosed with breast cancer when Sonia was eleven. Bert was already an alcoholic, and the mother was the only steady wage earner in the family. And she bought Bert his beer. When the mother died when Sonia was twelve, the family went hungry and went through multiple evictions. Bert was grieving, still drinking, already lung sick, and still useless. When Sonia was thirteen, she turned to prostitution to support the family. She had barely started menstruating. At first, she was dating high school guys who paid for sex at the end of the date. Then it was picking up drunks in bars and taking them to a flophouse motel next door. Then she found a pimp who brought johns to her at that motel. That way she didn't have to talk to them and pretend to seduce them. Sonia got pregnant when she was fifteen with the daughter who knocked on my door. Sonia knows that her daughter's father was a john. She just doesn't know which one or what his name might be. No names were ever shared.

Sonia found solace, anesthesia really, in harder and harder drugs. She was subject to bouts of depression, which just shows she had a good grasp of the reality of her situation. Oddly, she avoided a significant criminal record. The main reason that she had stayed out of prison was that she was never on probation. All her convictions were for prostitution, for which she had to do only a few days in county jail. If she had ever been placed on probation, she would have been drug tested regularly, and her use would have been detected and punished.

money for child care or let the boy stay home alone. She didn't even tell me about the problem at first. She seemed to me to be doing well, so I had moved on to trying to help other people.

Her daughter, who was then fifteen, called me one Sunday morning between worship services at my church. Her mom had run away again. It felt as if the devil were laughing at me. But things have been going so well, I said. So what, she asked, weary beyond her years.

I went on a search for Sonia all day and night that Sunday, hitting all of her former drug haunts. I flushed her out of one. She got away from me, because she was willing to drive a lot more dangerously than I was. She drove as if she were terrified of my catching her. As if I were the problem rather than the drugs. As if this was something I thought she had done to *me*, ruining one of *my* success stories. And she didn't want to be one of my stories any longer. Maybe she understood me better than I did. I left a note on a drug-house door, convinced she was hiding inside, a note that lectured her for giving into the demons of her past. Like I knew.

The next night, I found out that her fifteen-year-old daughter was pregnant. The devil was laughing some more. So it felt. And I don't really believe in the devil. But whether or not the devil exists doesn't depend upon whether I believe it. What I do believe is that believing in the devil just takes God and us off the hook for the broken way things are.

I wondered if Sonia would try to come back to work at the insurance company. I wanted to make some lame excuse to the employer, in case she would try. He told me that she had stormed out of the job on the day she ran away from her children. I think I remember that he told me that she broke something out of anger. Then she stomped out. I asked if he knew what brought that on. He confessed that he was telling Sonia's immediate supervisor about her background, about what she had been through, her past prostitution and drug use, how hard her life had been. He was telling her supervisor so he would be understanding and gentle with her. But some other employee overhead what was intended to be a private conversation. This employee told one person and then it spread the way things like that will. Sonia heard some whispering behind her back. How could she stay there? It made her feel small and strange and broken. She wouldn't be pitied. She wouldn't be judged. My friend was very remorseful this had happened. But he couldn't let her come back.

After that, I decided that I had made things worse by being so aggressive, that I had to wait for her to approach me for help. After months passed, I went looking for her again. I found the house where she and the

Maybe all we accomplished was to make Lupe feel, for a little while, that she was worth loving, that she was due protection. But in retrospect, I think that I was too intent upon fixing Sonia's and Lupe's lives. I was too hopeful that their lives could be fixed. I was too much about my accomplishing this.

I don't want to forget Lupe. I don't want to forget Sonia. I don't want to forget Sonia's children. What chance did any of them have to heal from their wounds? Summon up your empathy for a little girl who could depend upon the presence in her life of only one person, her granddad, who was utterly undependable in every other way. And for Sonia's children, who never knew whether their mother was coming home at the end of the day or whether she would sink back into the escape of drugs.

I can't condemn Sonia, even as the dominant narrative tells me to condemn, dismiss, and forget her. I can't blame her for any aspect of her plight. Yes, she repeatedly buried herself in the same grave. But she was born deep in it. Yes, she got out just a little but crawled right back in, and got out and crawled back in, and so on. And she pulled her children in with her. Down deep as she could get into her own heart and soul, she just didn't believe that she was due being anywhere else except that grave. Within the dominant narrative, she was due nothing. To try to be merciful to her was a waste of scarce resources and time. The same as with Lupe and Sonia's children.

But, as with Lupe, maybe just for a time Sonia realized how much I thought of her, that to me she was an infinitely valuable human being, that I loved her, and that she was and is due love. Under the counter-narrative of Jesus, the fruit that this may or may not bear is not up to me. It's up to God and Sonia. But under the counter-narrative of Jesus, loving and feeling loved are in themselves the greatest of fruits and the greatest of mercies. No mercy is ever wasted.

**

Raul Gutierrez (his actual name) is the brother I never had. He was a fellow student in seminary. After a year, he joined me as co-pastor of the inner-city church. Raul was born in a house with a dirt floor in Zacatecas, Mexico. He came to the U.S. as a boy with his father, an evangelical preacher. Raul became a U.S. citizen and graduated from college and then seminary here. He is, of course, bilingual. I was a lawyer and minister

I had talked to him for years. Morris was very successful in business. He was also extremely and sacrificially supportive of programs that would help children from economically poor families get out of their graves. He was director of the charitable foundation founded by a local professional athlete. Through the foundation, the athlete and Morris made charitable contributions to programs that helped poor children in need. There had been an article in the local newspaper recently about what we were trying to do at the church for poor children in our neighborhood. Morris's voice on the recorder said that the foundation was making an unsolicited $15,000 contribution to the church for our children's programs. This call came the very same day the idea of the coats and shoes had first occurred to Raul and me. The. Very. Same. Day.

The donation paid for the coats and shoes. In the mind of that neighborhood, our church became the place you came for help. We would regularly see families driving by in their torn-up cars and trucks, pointing at the church. See. That's the church. Those are the people. Once an eight year old I hadn't met before came to see me at the church. Someone had told him that he was surely going to hell because he had vandalized a car. I told him he was not. Then I asked him why he was asking me. "Because everyone says you know Jesus."

This out-of-the-blue, God-is-good donation of the $15,000 is a wonderful, heartwarming example of the mercy of exceptional people like Morris and the athlete within the dominant narrative I am so critical of here. Many would say it was a vindication of the system and rebuttal of my criticisms.

And there are so many effective charitable foundations funded and directed by the leading beneficiaries and advocates of the dominant narrative. Foundations started with a family's wealth, and beacons of hope within the general mercilessness of the dominant narrative. My Methodist Justice Ministry receives contributions from three of these foundations now.

But there is just not enough of this generous mercy, *which takes nothing away* from the generosity of the people who are so merciful. Are there not still millions of children trapped in poor neighborhoods? I am not writing here about governmental programs to deal with the issues of inequality and poverty, drugs and violence, and the breakdown of the family. Too many people who are in favor of such governmental programs fail to be generous with their own personal assets and abilities. Here, I am asking why, out of the billions of dollars in aggregate fortune of all the

**

We had a plague of gang violence in the neighborhood of the church. Rival gangs of males in their teens and early twenties. The gangs named themselves with three letters. *Barrio* in Spanish translates to neighborhood in English. And because *barrio* in Spanish is pronounced as if it were *varrio*, the first letter of the gang name was always a "V." So the gangs running our neighborhood were called "VDH" and "VRI" and "VMS," with lots of gang tags on walls.

There was a time when a new member's initiation into a gang would require him to drive the neighborhood with his vehicle headlights on bright and then to shoot at any car whose driver blinked their lights back at him. Then gang members started driving up to a rival gang member's home in the dead of night to shoot it up. One night a woman who had come to our church for food was killed as she lay sleeping in her bed, more than twenty bullets pouring through her house, one bullet hitting her in the head. Her son was a member of a rival gang. In retaliation for her murder, another home was shot up.

Members of our church led a demonstration march through the rival neighborhoods, trying to en-*courage* people to join in the protest and speak out against this random violence. Children were afraid to go to sleep in their own beds, but adults were still afraid to speak out for fear of retaliation. And people were afraid to tell the police who they knew was doing the shooting.

We worked with the local police gang unit to try to get people who knew the gunmen to confide in the police. Because the church had been providing free food, clothing, and financial assistance and even free legal advice to many families of the gang members, we were able to sit down separately with the leaders of each gang to appeal to them to stop putting innocent people in their cross-fire.

Then came the most extraordinary evening I have ever witnessed take place in any church. I had a good friend who was an attorney and a professional mediator. His tactic in lawsuit mediations was to talk and talk until the eyes of the parties rolled back in their heads and they would make concessions to get him to stop talking. I'm only kidding about that a little. But he was also a legendary, golden glove, heavy-weight boxer. Partly because he was the attraction, one winter's night about twenty members of both rival gangs met in my church's fellowship hall and hammered out some rules of engagement.

feared of all of the young men there had said nothing throughout the meeting. But then he spoke up as we were having one gang leave completely before the other. "Anybody messes with this church or hurts the priest or his friend answers to me personally," he announced to everyone there. "No one is going to hurt them," a leader of the other gang answered. Priest? Who was that? Then it hit me. The priest was me. They came from Roman Catholic families. So I was a priest. As much violence as they had committed, they were still capable of respecting the church of Jesus. They appreciated what the church was trying to do. They saw Jesus behind it.

The shootings between the gangs tailed off for a time, but then picked back up. But no more noncombatants were shot. We had no more shooting into darkened houses, no more gang initiations at the expense of innocent people. A very small step tending toward the kingdom of God.

The police gang unit complained to their commander that my friend and I obstructed justice in keeping them out of the meeting. These officers believed that a peaceful neighborhood would result simply from locking up every gang member. They were mistaken about that. For every gang member they locked up, another would be spawned by the smashed hopes produced by the dominant narrative.

The man who shot the mother lying in her bed may well have been in the church fellowship hall that night. When we asked the police to leave, we may have prevented them from identifying some gang members they had not previously made. We may have momentarily made it harder for the police to bring some of them to justice and to protect the community.

But all this depends upon how we define justice and how we decide what people are due. The man who shot the mother in her bed was due severe punishment from the criminal-justice system. But what else were the young men there due? What else were their families due?

The dominant narrative has a favorite put-down for those who aspire to be merciful. Bleeding heart. It is a phrase intended to discourage and devalue mercy. I aspire to be and have a bleeding heart. I wish my heart bled more than it does.

Why do young men join violent street gangs? Why do they subject themselves to that kind of violence? Based upon my getting to know many gang members during my time at that church, the answer lies in which young men join.

vulnerability at work, of the lowest ceiling on advancement, of a wage the family can't live on, of a body that breaks down after years of hard toil. Yet just like everyone else who is influenced by the dominant narrative, these young gang members wanted to be somebodies—respected and valued.

They want to be valued and respected members of a community, not just fungible, faceless, disposable costs of doing business, not just an economic competitor with a losing skin shade, accent, qualifications, and connections. What struck me most about the gangs themselves was what tight communities they were, almost a family. But they were communities that were mercilessly and criminally misdirected, projecting their resentments and frustrations on innocent people and on other gang members identical to themselves, assuring their own destruction and the insecurity of the neighborhood.

What are these young men due from others? According to the dominant narrative, nothing more than they were getting. In fact, they were due exactly what they were getting, no more, no less. And they aren't due any understanding or encouragement or a helping hand out of their graves. That is too much like mercy. No one is due mercy within this narrative. All they were due was the lives their parents lived and jail.

In my first story in chapter 1 of this book, I wrote about children who had little chance other than to climb on a conveyor belt of crime at the end of which was a prosecutor like I was, aiming to cage them until they were past their middle age. Here it was again.

I am not excusing the violence. There are men who are still in prison whom I put there because of their violence. But just putting violent young men one by one into prison will not stop the violence from continuing and growing from other young men born into the same merciless circumstances.

Bleeding heart. Consider closely that insult. How did we ever allow it to become an insult, even within the dominant narrative? Turning this into an insult is an attempt to discourage the mercy that the dominant narrative says is due to no one. Bleeding hearts can't run businesses and turn profits, says the dominant narrative. Bleeding hearts can't pursue progress and produce an increase in the GDP. Bleeding hearts can't defeat our nation's foes and secure our oil supplies and sea lanes. Bleeding hearts can't secure our borders and our streets. Bleedings hearts can't advance the work ethic among our class of cheap laborers. Turning bleeding heart into an insult is a transparent attempt to prevent us from seeing other people as members of a covenantal community, instead of just losers in

The father was smoking crack in the house, sometimes in the same room with the two children. When the mother asked him to stop, he would slap and punch her. She said she wanted a divorce. He said she would have to move out then. He was staying put. And the sons were staying with him.

I had no difficulty obtaining the emergency *ex parte* protective order from the court, which included a provision that the man leave the residence immediately.

But putting the husband and father out was more of a challenge.

Our local sheriff's department and city police force will not execute such a put-out order. So there can be a long delay until the abuser actually gets out. The order has to be personally served upon him. Then, when he refuses to comply, a separate motion to hold him in contempt for failing to get out must be filed, a hearing on the motion has to be set, the motion and the notice of hearing has to be personally served upon him, the hearing has to held, and if he is held in contempt he will still likely to be given the chance to get out within a certain time before going to jail for willful disobedience of a court order. So an abuser can thumb his nose at the law for up to a month before he actually has to obey the original order and get out. Where was the woman to live during that period? It was just another reason for an abused woman not to turn to the law for protection.

I went to the house to serve the order on the abuser with the gentleman I was using as my processor server at that time. The good news is that he was a former U.S. deputy marshal. The not so good news was that he was in his 70s and was just returning to work from an illness. He did not carry a weapon, and I sure didn't. The man we were serving and trying to put out was 30 years old and had a number of criminal convictions for violence.

We found the man asleep in his bed. It was 4 in the afternoon. The former marshal woke him up, explained who we were and what he was being served with. The abuser cursed us and said he wasn't accepting any document and for us to get out.

I then told him that I was his wife's lawyer, that I was a free lawyer, that I was also a Methodist minister, and that my legal work was part of a ministry. I told him that I had filed divorce papers on behalf of his wife that day, that this protective order was signed by the court, and required him to get out of the house immediately and to stay at least 200 yards away or face contempt of court and jail time.

of man he ought to be. But what he is due, to be made a better person, a person who is merciful to his family and to himself, is much more than the punishment that the dominant narrative would provide.

**

So many times in the last thirteen years with the Methodist Justice Ministry, we have convinced a judge to deny fathers any contact with their children because of repeated and unreformed abusiveness, untreated mental illness, and alcohol and drug abuse. In most of those cases, that man had witnessed as a boy another man abusing his mother and had even been abused himself. And he had been taught in a lost subculture that the tests of a man are control, abuse and violence. So many abusive men feel so impotent in their work and in their place in the society that they claim potency and value in their lives, assert that they are somebodies, by terrorizing their innocent partners and children. Home with their families feels like the one place that they can wield the dominance that the dominant narrative teaches is valuable. So often their anger and projected dissatisfactions with themselves, coupled with addiction and mental illness, get out of control. The lives of these men have often been tragic and manifestly unjust, inflicting wounds upon them that they were not due. So the boy becomes the father of the man.

I am not excusing the terrible conduct. We try to protect the women and the children. Much less is the woman due the terrible abuse received from the wounded man to whom she should be able to look most for love, support, and protection. And even less are the children due this violent home. So the justice of denying the father any access to the family is a kind of mercy to the woman and children as well. But human justice and mercy rarely fit together that neatly. Most often, the children still love the father deeply and have an almost inexhaustible capacity and urge to forgive him. They feel a hole in their lives when even an abusive father is taken away. Often the children believe deep in their minds and souls that they, the children, are somehow to blame for the violence and exile of the dad. And the mother loses the man to help in at least some parenting needs, which can be a particularly huge loss to a poor, working mother. Mercy might give the man another chance, albeit regulated. But is he due that chance as a matter of justice, after his failed second and third

on a burner in the bathroom of their house. She remembers riding her bicycle around her neighborhood one day and returning home to see her house on fire. Her mother had caused the fire by cooking meth. She remembers that was the incident that put her into foster care.

While Mary was in foster care for five years or so, her mother married, became clean for a time, and gave birth to three more children. Her mother regained custody of Mary. Then Mary's mother went back to meth, and the husband abandoned Mary and her half-siblings. While the mother was out looking for sex with high-school boys in exchange for meth, Mary was at home taking care of her three half-siblings. The family lived for a time in a trailer and when the mother brought boys home to have sex for drugs, Mary and her younger siblings could hear the sounds of sex through the thin walls. Mary was so devoted to her siblings, spending so much of her time mothering and protecting them, that she was in danger of failing her senior year in high school. A teacher convinced Mary to move out of her mother's trailer and in with a friend until she could graduate. The mother then took the three half-siblings, aged seven through five, to a distant relative in a distant city and dumped them. Soon, the mother was in prison again for methamphetamine possession.

Mary graduated from high school, moved alone to a nearby city, enrolled in junior college, and was working her way toward nursing school at two waitressing jobs. She had no help at all. She was alone in her rented home. Then she found out that the people on whom her mother had dumped her siblings had dumped them, too. Mary picked them up, took them in, quit school, sold her laptop to buy the children clothes, and became their mother. She was nineteen at the time.

When Mary first took possession of these siblings, she had no legal right to enroll them in school or to make medical decisions for them. The children were way behind on their vaccinations and one of the children needed psychiatric and psychological diagnosis and intervention for learning and behavioral issues. Mary needed to obtain legal custody of her siblings to be able to make parental decisions. The Justice Ministry was able to obtain this custody for her. But Mary and her siblings also needed a functioning vehicle, a healthy and safe place to live, a job that paid a living wage for Mary, and a way for Mary to continue her education. The MJM and my church were also able to help her obtain these things.

Mary is not only, as I already described her, beautiful, sweet, bright, loving, and hard-working. I left out one thing. She is also Anglo. Her

declined to seek custody. Her siblings could have been placed into the foster care system. But there they likely would have been separated. Carlota was as poor as could be. She could reasonably have decided that she was not able to be a parent. As a legal custodian of four children, with the *legal* obligations to feed, clothe, shelter, educate, discipline, and obtain medical care for them, she was not going to have the time and opportunity to get the necessary training to make more than minimum wage. I discussed all this at length with her before she asked us to obtain legal custody for her. She really didn't hesitate. She felt that her siblings were due to be raised by someone in their family who loved them. They were not due the trauma of losing their father and then the shock of the death of their mother. They were definitely not then due the further trauma of being split up and raised by people whom they did not know, and who might or might not love them. So when we took Carlota on as a client, we knew we would be providing even more material and financial support to her and the children than we usually provide. We knew that we would be taking our own responsibility to stand with Carlotta. Not under the dominant narrative but under the counter-narrative of Jesus, she and her siblings were due all the mercy we could give them as a matter of justice.

Carlota has a bit of a learning disability. Like Mary, Carlota is also cute, sweet, caring and hard-working. But she is not Anglo, so we have had a much harder time getting help for Carlota and her four Hispanic-American siblings from generous insiders. We weren't able to get Carlota a good job that paid a living wage with an empathetic boss and good health insurance.

Two of Carlotta's siblings have a learning disability. One is starting to wander down the wrong roads. Carlota works behind the counter at a Taco Bueno. She makes seventy-five cents more than minimum wage. Her work provides her with no set hours and no benefits. She and her siblings survive on her meager wages plus food stamps. Her boss does not care what hours she needs to be home to care for her siblings or that the job doesn't pay enough for her to live even with the SNAP. If Carlota quit, her boss could quickly find a thousand other economically poor girls to take her place. The work schedule is put out for the boss's convenience and the needs of the business. So Carlota cannot be home consistently to ensure that her siblings come home from school on time, do their homework, turn off the TV and videogames, and stay away from the peers they need to avoid. Carlota can't afford child care, so the oldest sibling is supposed to be the sitter. That sibling is the one going down the wrong road.

Carlota needed daily help. She met a young man who lived in the apartment complex. He had himself been in foster care throughout his teenaged years. He was the same age as Carlotta. He started hanging around the apartment and made friends with the siblings. He was allergic to employment, so had no place else to be. But Carlota was very grateful and came to depend upon him. Carlota was a young woman with a young person's needs. The young man started staying overnight, sleeping on the couch. Then he made his way into Carlotta's bed. He was persistent. At first she refused his advances. But he sulked and threatened to end his help. She gave in. She got pregnant. She gave birth. Then there were five children for her to take care of with a father and babysitter who could not find a hoe handle to fit his hand.

Unlike with Mary, we have not been able to find people to support and encourage Carlota and her family. I guess Carlota and her siblings are not as deserving. Such is the hit and miss character of charity within the dominant narrative. Mercy, after all, is only optional. And these children of Carlotta's are not due much at all as a matter of justice, according to the dominant narrative.

In ten years, we are betting that Mary will be a registered nurse and that her siblings will be productive and happy, given the mothering and example she has given them. In ten years, we are afraid that Carlota will still be working in the fast-food industry. Her siblings and her child . . . what can we reasonably hope for them?

**

"Cathy" was thirty-three years old when she hung herself. She climbed onto a kitchen table, looped a rope over a ceiling beam, tied the rope around her neck, and jumped off the table. It probably took her a while to lose all consciousness. Her three-year-old daughter watched as Cathy did all this.

Cathy had two other children, ten and eight. The three year old ran to get them. The ten year old later recounted that they arrived to see Cathy's body twitching at the end of the rope, her legs kicking, and her face blue. They called Cathy's mother. When Cathy's mother arrived, Cathy was already dead though her body was still warm. All three children were shooed out of the room when the EMT techs cut the body down.

None of the fathers was fit to take custody of these children. None wanted custody. None had been paying their previously ordered child support. All three of the fathers had multiple other children by other women who were not their wives.

The Justice Ministry was able to get legal custody of all three children for the grandparents. Through the help of one of our board members, we were able to get this family into a larger home and to provide them with used furniture. We were able to obtain fresh orders from the court requiring each father to pay their current child support and their child-support arrearages to the grandparents. None of them have paid a penny. A child support order is merely a piece of paper when its subject is a parent who works off the books and moves from job to job.

Years later, the children still suffer from serious emotional disruptions. The grandparents still can't find a responsive pediatric psychiatrist who takes Medicaid.

What are these children due within the dominant narrative, and from whom? Nothing from no one except their suffering and overmatched grandparents. All they can hope for is occasional, optional mercy.

Given the pervasiveness and power of the dominant narrative, what will these children ever be equipped to do or be? Given the depression that is a plague in their household and their own trauma, will they ever be able to work productively and to acquire the stuff and pleasure to be respected and successful within the dominant narrative? Will they ever even be "deserving" of help under that narrative?

**

"Abigail" was thirty-four years old and the mother of eight children. Three of these had been placed in foster care by CPS, and Abigail's most recent maternity had been legally terminated. Custody of one of the other children had been granted to that child's father who lived out of state.

Abigail's remaining four children were a girl aged ten, a girl aged eight, a boy aged two, and a boy aged four months. The identity of the fathers of the girls were unknown to Abigail. The father of the two-year-old boy was in prison in another state. The identity of the father of the four-month-old boy was known to Abigail, but his whereabouts were not. This father had choked Abigail when she was in the hospital recovering

child with Anne. Abigail never paid Anne or her family. Anne came to consider these children part of her family.

When CPS was called in after the father of the youngest child choked Abigail in the hospital just after the delivery, Anne was referred to us to help her obtain legal custody of all four children.

So twelve people lived in Anne's house, including these four children. To call that house modest would be flattery. In winter, the inside of that house seemed colder to me than the outside. In summer, the inside seemed hotter than the outside. It is crammed full with human beings at any given moment. And it is crammed full of love. When you are invited in, the very first thing you notice is that the interior walls are covered, top to bottom, side to side, every room, with framed, black and white photos of all the children who live there. And the photos of Abigail's four children are as numerous and prominent as the children of Anne's daughter Rachel or the children of Anne's sister.

Anne is completely unselfconscious of her generosity. Those children had no one else besides her. "God placed them in my path. How could I pass by? Now I love them."

The dominant narrative would call Anne a fool and a sap. None of these strangers are due anything from Anne. By taking these children in, less foolish people would say that Anne is stealing resources and time from her actual children and grandchildren.

But the dominant narrative has no soul and no heart. Anne is one of the happiest and most satisfied persons I have ever known. She is merciful and just at the same time. She is adored by *all* of those children and her entire family. And by all of us at the Methodist Justice Ministry.

**

"Julia" was born in Mexico City and brought by her mother and father to the United States when she was three. She has not been back to Mexico since she was brought here. She attended public schools here, graduating high school. When her graduating class took a cruise to Cancun as a graduation celebration, she could not go. She was still undocumented, "an illegal alien" within the system. After the cruise, Julia would not have been able to get back through U.S. customs and back to what is undeniably her home here in the U.S. And after her graduation, despite a 4.0 grade point average but without a social security number, she always

and had served as a kind of haven for the children when James was being violent. Aunt Julia was someone in whom the children, and particularly the three girls, felt they could confide.

Annette found a new man named "Jake." Jake had at least two biological children of his own by two different women he had not married. He had been ordered to pay child support for each of those children but had refused. Jake was unemployed. He had been convicted twice of marijuana possession and of unlawful carrying of a firearm. Jake moved into the apartment where Annette lived with her five children. As soon as he did, he cut off all contact between Julia, Emilia, and the children. Julia would call Annette to ask to speak to the children, but there was never an answer.

When this was unfolding, Aunt Julia was 28 years old, single and still undocumented.

Four months into the relationship between Annette and Jake, Julia drove by their apartment. She saw the children through a second-story bedroom window. The oldest child, a boy who was then twelve, tried to mouth words to Julia. Julia yelled at him to open the window. He just shook his head. Julia could see the youngest child, a boy seven years old, crying in the background. Julia went to the apartment door and knocked. There was no answer. Julia went back to the window and gestured for them to open the front door. The oldest boy again shook his head no. Julia yelled, "Why not?" The boy yelled back, "We're locked in the bedroom."

Julia went to Annette's old employment at the parking garage but was told that she no longer worked there. So Julia went back to Annette's apartment and waited.

Jake arrived at the apartment two hours later. Julia intercepted him before he could climb the stairs to the apartment door. "Why are the children locked in a bedroom?"

"Who are you?"

"I'm their aunt. I'm their father's sister."

"I'm their father now. You can't talk to them. Stay the f*** away from here or I will call the police." He went into the apartment and slammed the door in Julia's face.

Julia waited for Annette to come home. More hours passed. A progression of men went to the door of the apartment, were let in, remained only a few moments, and left. Then Julia saw Annette walking to the apartment from a bus stop. Julia intercepted her. "Annette, I was here earlier and the children told me through the bedroom window that they

When Julia asked why he would lock them in, Annette said she did not know. But the oldest child, the twelve year old boy, said he believed that Jake had drugs hidden somewhere in the apartment that he did not want the children to find. He said that when Jake was in the apartment when the children were there after school, random people would come in and out. When they knocked on the door, Jake would order all the children into the back bedroom while he was dealing with the visitors. The twelve year old thought he was selling drugs. Jake always had a wad of cash, but no job.

Julia asked Annette why she had tolerated this, and why she hadn't left or called the police before. Annette tried to tell Julia that Jake was a good person, and that she loved him. Julia told her that she had to choose between that man and her children. Annette said she had, which was why she was there.

Jake was arrested and charged with assault against Annette. A protective order was issued by a magistrate, directing Jake to stay away from Annette and the five children for sixty days. Jake found another place to live. Annette went back to her apartment with the children, and Julia started sleeping there as well at the two older children's request.

While Julia was staying with them, she noticed that Annette was distant and uninvolved with her children, barely paying them any attention. Julia was the one mothering them. Then Annette started coming home later and later, claiming that she had been working. Then she didn't come home at all. Two days later, Annette left a message on Julia's cell phone. She said she couldn't live without Jake. She was the one violating the protective order so Julia should not call the police. She said she would be coming to pick up her children in a few weeks, when things had calmed down and Jake was ready for them to come live with them again.

Julia told the oldest two children about her mother's message. They were afraid of going back to live in any home with Jake in it. They started opening up more to Julia and Emilia about what Jake had been doing. Jake called them "punks," "dummies" and "leaches." He threatened to knock out their teeth if they disobeyed him, even the youngest children. He told all of the children: "What happens here stays here. If you tell anyone what is happening here, I will shoot your mother and Julia. If you tell anyone about being locked in your room, you will see what will happen." The twelve year old described seeing Jake with a handgun with a scope. The three oldest children told Julia that when Jake locked them in the back bedroom, he left a piece of paper on top of the outside of

And the employer knew that undocumented workers couldn't complain without fearing deportation.

Emilia had obtained a resident visa years before. She could work legally. No visa had been obtained for Julia because the lawyer had neglected Julia's case, and the family had no money to pay for another lawyer. Emilia was 49 years old. She worked on an assembly line, making about $9 an hour.

The CPS investigator returned to say that Annette had agreed to a safety plan placing possession of the children with Julia and Emilia for now and limiting Annette to visitation with the children supervised by Julia. She said that Annette agreed to this only because the children would be split up and placed in foster care with strangers if Annette did not agree. There were no other family members to take them in voluntarily.

Fresh on Julia's mind was her conversation with her boss. So Julia asked the investigator if CPS would be providing her and her mother with some supplemental income to help them feed and care for the children. No, said the investigator. The state can only pay foster families, not actual family members who voluntarily take possession. Can we be a foster family so we can receive some reimbursement? No, said the investigator. Why not? Because you and your mother have already taken the children in outside the foster system, and because the state wants to save money. Julia asked if they could apply for food stamps while they had possession of the children. Not until you obtain legal custody from a court, said the investigator. Can Annette be ordered to pay us child support to help us provide for her children? No, said the investigator. Not unless you obtain legal custody from a court. When can we do that? Not until we give Annette and Jake a chance to take our classes on parenting and family violence. Can you require Annette to give us her food stamps for the children? No, but you can ask her.

Annette and Jake refused to take their required classes. Annette lied that she was leaving Jake, but she was caught in the lie. Jake refused to let Annette give Julia the food stamp card for the children.

Julia, Emilia and the children survived, barely, until the Methodist Justice Ministry was able to get them legal custody. They survived on Julia's and Emilia's meager pay and by tightening their belts. And Julia took out a title loan on her car, which required her to pay back over time about 600 percent of what she had borrowed. That's not an error. About 600 percent of the principal she borrowed.

would suffer. Within the dominant narrative, Julia, Emilia, and these children are due nothing more from us than the firm enforcement of the law without exception or mercy.

And the apologists of those who benefit the most from the dominant narrative use it mercilessly to scapegoat Julia and those in her status. To stoke up fear of "them" who are no threat. Of Julia! There are only so many benefits of our society to be divided up, the advocates for the dominant narrative say. This isn't just an *agón*. This is a zero-sum *agón*. For every benefit that Julia received within our system, one of us would be deprived of what was due us, they say. Nevermind that Julia receives no such monetary benefit. And she isn't depriving one of us of a job that pays less than even the legal minimum wage because none of "us" would want or take it.

But from the people of God formed by the counter-narrative of God and Jesus, what are Julia, Emilia and the children due? What is Annette due? What is James due?

**

"Nancy's" parents were methamphetamine addicts. Her father sold meth from the family home as Nancy and her brother were growing up there. The father injected or smoked his profits. So the family remained poor. Her father went to prison repeatedly. Her mother "Maggie" managed to avoid any criminal charges. The family moved from rented house to rented house. Their home was always dirty, cluttered and reeking of cigarette smoke. And there were always a lot of dogs and roaches.

Nancy's brother started using meth and cocaine when he was fourteen. He dropped out of school in the ninth grade. He turned to burglary to raise the money to buy his drugs. His parents were hardly in a position to push him in the right direction. The only line that they drew for him was that he couldn't get any of his drugs from them. When he started stealing from their inventory, they kicked him out. He went quickly from couch surfing at friend's homes to juvenile detention. Shortly after he turned eighteen, he landed in adult prison for the first time. He was eventually paroled, of course had no job prospects, and turned to armed robbery as a career. At the age of twenty-eight, he was sentenced to fifteen years in prison. By that time, he had fathered a son. The mother of his son was mentally ill and an addict.

discharge under less than honorable conditions. The Air Force offered her that, instead of a dishonorable or a bad conduct discharge, to get her out quickly.

She went to live in Virginia with another Airman also just discharged for drug use, a man she had abused Oxycodone with while they were in. She got pregnant. She used heroin while she was pregnant. The baby was born addicted to heroin and remained in the hospital for two weeks after birth, going through withdrawal. Virginia Child Protective Services were called, and Nancy's newborn, a little girl, was placed in foster care. Nancy's maternal rights were soon terminated when she would not return to rehab and would not quit using.

She was twenty-one years old.

She returned to her mother's home because she had no place else to go. The tension between Nancy and Maggie was intense. Maggie knew firsthand what was driving Nancy to use. But when Maggie pleaded with her, trying to give her the benefit of her own experience, Nancy responded that her mother had no right to lecture her given her own past and the childhood that her mother had inflicted on her.

Nancy's self-loathing and her resentment of her mother contributed to her escaping to a succession of men who used her body in exchange for meth. Then her loathing for herself, for her weakness, for her past, her present and her hopeless future, and for the men who used her body would boil over into drugged arguments, insults, and mutual assaults. With fresh bruises and choke marks, she would return to her mother's home, having nowhere else to go, but more resentful, sullen and self-loathing than before.

Once when she returned to Maggie's home, Nancy found that she was pregnant. Maggie insisted that Nancy tell the father. The father was so moved to learn that he was to be a father for the first time that he resolved to sober up. Nancy resolved to do so as well for the sake of her child. She didn't want to have this child taken from her by the state. So Nancy and the father moved in with the father's mother. The father went to work at a Subway, eventually working himself up to manager. Nancy stayed with the father's mother until she delivered, taking some classes at a local community college. Nancy had a normal pregnancy and was drug free throughout. Her life was enlivened with some hope for the first time since she had been in the car wreck. She hoped that she and the father would marry, that she would be able to get her associate's degree, and that they would have a normal family life.

plants in the inventory. The friend did require a drug test of Nancy's scalp hair, which will show any drug use for the previous four months plus. Nancy's test showed no drug use, and she was hired.

No one in that store knew her or her past. She was hard working, smart, and grateful to be working. There was a lot of turn-over at that store, which included a grocery, and she was soon promoted to the manager of the garden shop. In a year's time her uncle's friend was made a manager over seven stores. He promoted Nancy to night manager of her store. The store was open 24 hours a day. Nancy worked from 8 p.m. to 4 am. The grocery section was restocked beginning at 4 am every morning. Nancy was in charge of a crew that readied the merchandise for the restocking. She was given a decent salary with health insurance. And she had a real prospect of being made an overall store manager, able to work days instead of nights.

Her second child had never been far from her thoughts. I was introduced to Nancy through her mother, Maggie, whom we had helped obtain legal custody of her grandson. Nancy's income had recently risen above our income eligibility ceiling, which is 125 percent of federal poverty line. But I had the prerogative to waive that ceiling in selective cases. And in reality she could not afford a lawyer to obtain visitation rights with her daughter. I was so taken by her story—all she had been through in her life, how she had cleaned herself up, and how hard she was working. Nancy had made so many very bad mistakes. But I felt she had been more sinned against than sinning. And I felt she and her daughter were due our help and encouragement. Her daughter deserved to have a relationship with her mother. We filed suit and were able to obtain for Nancy shared custody of her daughter and regular possession rights.

Nancy's little girl was so very happy to have Nancy back in her life. Nancy was doing so well. It seemed that she had defeated her past. I suggested to her that she had a great deal to offer people who had been trapped in addiction. She had overcome such a difficult past and addiction that she could help other people to overcome their pasts, and their addictions.

More than a year later, I went by her the store to see how she was doing. We had moved onto other people's crises and had heard nothing from her or her mother. I was told that she had quit her job at the store three months earlier. I hoped she had found a better job with better pay, and better hours. Or maybe she had gone back to school to become a drug-addiction counselor. So I called her mother.

counselors, recovering alcoholics and addicts, and people still abusing alcohol and drugs at the time. Clearly, by accident of birth Nancy had a genetic predisposition to addiction. Her exposure to her mother and father's drug use had made her own use more thinkable.

I knew from my past friendship with Nancy that she had a deep layer of self-doubt and self-hatred. She could never trust when things were going well for her. She didn't believe that she was due any happiness from life. She couldn't trust herself, and she couldn't trust the goodness of life itself. It was as if she had to sabotage things before she was somehow discovered as undeserving. She had to ditch that good life before that good life would ditch her.

And I believe there was another aspect of it. This dominant narrative's emphasis upon pleasure teaches that we must go from high to high, from extraordinary experience to extraordinary experience, to be truly alive. Just look at the advertising that drowns us. We need the thrills of life—the intense pleasure of this delicious, cheap, unhealthy food, this new truck or automobile that will take us into beautiful vistas for rendezvous with beautiful people, this resort vacation, this cruise, this wine, and this bedroom furniture. We need the beer of "the most interesting man in the world" to have an interesting life. And we live vicariously through athletes, the intensity and the immediacy of winning and losing, and the adoration the athletes receive. Or we live vicariously through celebrities who have talent for nothing other than attracting media attention. We are taught to mistake transient intensity for the enduring intimacy for which we really yearn in our souls. In my experience these yearnings for the immediacy of high after high are particularly strong for addicts. For a part of Nancy, when life was going so well—a decent job with an adequate income, benefits and a decent future, and mothering her daughter day to day with all those satisfactions and joys—life wasn't going so well at all. The highs weren't there. There was no risk. One day slid into another.

After I brought Nancy back to her uncle's, she worked there for a time and cleaned up again. She contacted the father of her daughter and arranged to see her. I was there when Nancy saw the little girl for the first time in months, and that child was so very happy to see her mommy.

The father had left his wife and other child. He had the same job as before, but was using meth periodically again. Nancy moved into his apartment to be able to be with her daughter. She started using meth with him. Nancy and the father got into another drug fight one night. The daughter, now two years old, was cowering in the bedroom while daddy

to call him her uncle. Then he started writing her letters, saying that he wanted to take care of her.

Lakeisha's mother moved to my city with a new boyfriend. Their old home in New Orleans was still uninhabitable because of the hurricane. The mother, boyfriend, and Lakeisha stayed in an extended-stay motel. Byron tracked them there, and moved into the same complex.

Lakeisha's mother started using crack cocaine again. She used so much and so often, as she had in New Orleans, that she was disabled. The mother was not paying any attention to Lakeisha. Byron took this opportunity to take over the care of Lakeisha. He fed her, bought her clothes, and drove her to school and back. Byron had found a job working night shift as a dispatcher for a trucking company. He was contributing money to Lakeisha's mother for her own needs. When the mother had the chance to return to New Orleans, Byron essentially bought Lakeisha, who was then fourteen. Byron paid the mother a sum of money and received a written document giving him the power to make all parental decisions in the mother's absence.

Byron found them a secluded house set well back from the street by a large yard. He made Lakeisha drop out of school. He drove away her friends. He isolated her completely. Her older brothers in New Orleans did not know she was living with Byron. Her mother told her brothers that she was living with a friend of hers. Lakeisha had never learned to drive, and Byron kept it that way. He denied her access to the internet, email, or any social media. They never went out. Lakeisha had grown up in so much poverty, a cocaine addict for a mother and an absent father, that she was happy at first with the arrangement. Byron was the caring father she had never had.

It started with oral sex performed by her on him. She was completely inexperienced sexually before then. Byron groomed her by having Lakeisha watch pornography. Byron waited until Lakeisha was sixteen before he had intercourse with her. He was impatient and insistent before then. But she was afraid, and he let her refuse. He finally raped her one night. She was crying, angry, and hurting. When he kept forcing himself on her, she was unresponsive and then withdrawn. He lowered her defenses by telling her that God had sent her to him and him to her, that God meant for her to be his wife and for him to be her husband and to free her from poverty. And as the wife God had selected for him, it was her duty to have sex with him. When she objected that he was too old and she was too

man named "Alec" who was just a few years older than she. She explained her plight to him. So they arranged for him to help her escape Byron.

Lakeisha successfully fled with the children to Alec's apartment. This was her escape haven. She was ignorant of the existence of local women's shelters. She was still in the same plight as she was in New Orleans, unable to find work and provide for her children. Alec was a good-looking, strong, young man. He was pleased and surprised to see that Lakeisha was an attractive young woman. The inevitable eventually happened.

After three weeks, Lakeisha telephoned Byron and told him where she and the children were. He came over and pounded on the apartment door, demanding the return of his wife and children. Alec faced him down and told him never to return. Byron called the police. The police came, found that the children were in good health, told Byron that Lakeisha had as much right to possession of the children as he did, and that he would have to file suit in family court to obtain custody.

Byron filed a custody suit and had the constable serve Lakeisha. At the initial hearing, both parties represented themselves. Byron lied that Lakeisha was making money as a stripper and as a prostitute, and that she had moved her children in with her pimp. Lakeisha was overwhelmed by the court process and was unable to tell her side of the story. The associate judge granted primary custody of the children to Byron, granted Lakeisha only supervised visitation, and ordered her to pay child support.

Lakeisha was crying outside the courtroom after the hearing. A compassionate family attorney tried to comfort her. Though this attorney did not offer to represent her for free, she did tell Lakeisha that she had a right to request a new hearing before the district judge. The court coordinator helped her fill out the demand.

Lakeisha and Byron appeared before the district judge for a new hearing. When it became evident to the judge that Lakeisha was Byron's victim, she reset the hearing and had her court coordinator call the Justice Ministry.

I filed for divorce. At the rescheduled hearing, it was my pleasure to cross-examine Byron. I had arranged for a detective from the police department of the city where Lakeisha and Byron first lived and had sex to be in the courtroom. And I led Byron through all of the elements of proof of what is commonly known as statutory rape, all of which Byron arrogantly admitted.

The judge, of course, returned the children to Lakeisha. Byron was restricted to visits with the children supervised at the visitation center

housing. Every month was a financial crisis. The Justice Ministry paid their rent for months.

The trauma of her past, the stress of the poverty, the crowded two-bedroom apartment housing two adults and four children, and the constant needs of the ill newborn were too much for Lakeisha. She couldn't sleep. She began to lose her temper with Alec and her children unpredictably. She would lose control and throw things at Alec in the presence of the children. There was so much violence in the home that Child Protective Services became involved. Alec had to supervise all of Lakeisha's contact with her children, which kept him out of the job market. Lakeisha was referred by CPS for psychological assessment and was diagnosed with bipolar disorder and Post Traumatic Stress Disorder from the trauma of her entire history. She was required to attend parenting classes and anger-management counseling, and to take medication. She completed all of her services, and CPS closed its case and its supervision.

Then she got pregnant again. Alec left her. I put Lakeisha and her children on the bus to New Orleans. She had no place else to go, even though Louisiana is no place for her.

Lakeisha had been a victim since she was born. Her mother was a crack addict and a crack dealer. Her father was never involved or supportive in any way. A hurricane drove them out of their hometown and into the arms of a twisted stranger. Lakeisha was essentially a victim of sex trafficking. Her mother sold her to a twisted man thirty years her senior, who made her a sex slave, not a wife. When she woke up to all that had been done to her and ran for freedom, she also ran back to poverty. The man who did most of this to her has thwarted the law because of an unmotivated assistant district attorney or an uncaring grand jury, and an ineffective interstate child-support collection system. And Lakeisha has a child with an ongoing heart problem and her own mental-health issues. Now the father of her last child has bailed on her. So Lakeisha has taken her children into the home of a crack addict and dealer where she will remain until she meets another man who takes her and her children in and gets her pregnant.

How much of what happened to Lakeisha was due to her? How does the culture created by the dominant narrative respond to the utter injustice and mercilessness of her life? Food stamps and section 8 housing, if the waiting isn't too long. Medicaid. Nothing that will change her plight. Just maintenance in her poverty.

any child support. All four fathers were in prison when the Justice Ministry filed the custody suits and obtained a court order appointing Carolyn managing conservator of these children. And we helped her with some of the material needs of the children.

I'm telling this story because it is one of the most frequent scenarios we confront, although usually it's grandparents, not great grandparents, who take custody.

We are seeing an epidemic of drug abuse by poor, young parents. We try to protect and place in protective homes child after child who is the product of a drug-induced hook-up between virtual strangers. We have had hundreds of cases in which a child was born addicted to drugs. We have interviewed, negotiated with, or cross-examined hundreds of parents who were abusing drugs, some while they were pregnant. The dominant narrative just condemns and discards these parents. And within this narrative their *conduct* is worthy of condemnation and deterrence. But the dominant narrative is as heedless of the welfare of the children as are the parents. The narrative's version of justice means no help or intervention is due them—parent or child. According to the dominant narrative, mercy is ineffective and undeserved. Ironically, there is a hopelessness, a cynicism, and even a nihilism in all this behavior and response—both the drug use and the lack of help and intervention from the culture shaped by the dominant narrative.

Much of this drug use is anesthesia against the pain of feeling worthless and hopeless within the culture. These young parents know they have no valued place. The dominant culture communicates through its entire media and through all its mouthpieces that a person's value and worth comes from the acquisition of stuff and shallow pleasures, and the honor that comes with those. Gratification must be immediate. As I have written, this dominant narrative doesn't really value and honor hard work at an honest job. The only jobs available to these young people are unvalued and belittling. They don't pay nearly enough for one person to survive. Many of the drug users are also involved in selling drugs to get stuff and pleasure.

An addict mistakes intensity and immediacy for intimacy. The entire dominant culture *prefers* intensity and immediacy to intimacy. The narrative teaches us to prefer stuff and shallow pleasures over community.

What are these children due within the dominant narrative? Or from within the world being created by the counter-narrative of Jesus?

because her pay was barely enough to survive. Her employer provided her with no health insurance. While she was recovering, she was fired and told she could reapply when she was able to work again. When she recovered as much as she was going to, she had some lingering pain, so the employer would not take her back. The employer was able to hire a younger replacement at an even lower wage. She had no family left. She was evicted from her apartment for non-payment of rent. So she moved into a walk-in shelter for the homeless, one in which guests cannot stay during the day. Most sleep on mats on the floor, side to side and head to feet with the people sleeping around them.

When I met Jane, she was still living in that shelter. When she applied for a new job, she had to put down the shelter address as her residence and had to give the shelter's phone as a call-back number. When a prospective employer called and heard that she was living at the night shelter, they immediately lost interest in hiring her. She has been out of work so long that she is now trapped there.

This kind of story is far more common than the dominant narrative would have us believe. According to the dominant narrative, Jane is homeless because she deserves it. According to this narrative, Jane is homeless because she is lazy. According to the dominant narrative, Jane is merely a loser of the *agón*.

People prey upon the homeless in their need. In my city, the homeless are funneled into one neighborhood because all of the services and shelters are located there, and because they are shunned and coerced into being there. I would say that the homeless are treated like stray dogs, except that more people will help a stray dog than will help a homeless person. The fast-food places, gas stations, and convenience stores in "their" neighborhood regularly cheat homeless workers. They promise to pay them less than minimum wage. Then they pay them less than the amount they promised. Or they fail to pay them at all.

Almost all the able-bodied, homeless males in my city have used a private, for-profit labor pool operator to find work. The office is located on the edge of the homeless neighborhood. Homeless people line up well before dawn every day to try to be picked for work. The work is often "walking paper"—walking door to door in a distant neighborhood, stuffing flyers into front doors, with the promise of being paid pennies per page stuffed. So the operator looks for people who can walk fast and long.

One labor pool operator preyed upon alcoholics. This operator had contracts with local, professional, athletic venues to clean the spectator

service" to the sheep. After all, who else was supplying the thirsty sheep with water?

Second, a story.

We at the Justice Ministry represented a young woman named "Louise." Louise was thirty and had a son who was almost ten and a daughter who was twelve. The father of the children was "Roger." Roger refused to marry Louise. He supported Louise and the two children intermittently, just often enough to keep them dependent upon him. Louise had a high-school education but was unable to make the kind of money on her own to cover child care to enable her to work full time. So she needed his support, as unreliable as it was. Roger would show up at Louise's door with some cash, demand to spend the night in her bed, ignore the children and leave. She suspected he had the same relationship with other women who were also mothers of his children.

Roger was an alcoholic and a drug abuser. Even when he showed up drunk and high, she still felt she had to let him in to receive his money. He was verbally and physically abusive to her in front of the children. When the son started imitating Roger's behavior, Louise was moved to act. She called the police when he assaulted her the next time. She moved herself and her children to another apartment, the location of which was unknown to him. She carried through on the criminal prosecution. He pled guilty to the assault and received 90 days in jail, which he served on weekends. And she applied to the local District Attorney's Protective Order Unit. The DA's office obtained a two-year Protective Order for Louise. And the Unit referred Louise to the Justice Ministry so we could enforce the Protective Order when Roger inevitably violated it, and so we could obtain a child-support court order requiring Roger to pay a set amount of monthly support so Louise could try to make a new life free of him.

When Louise came to the Justice Ministry, she had not been able to work full time and her part-time job was low pay. Because Roger had not provided any money to her for many months, Louise had fallen behind in her rent payments. She and her children were in danger of being evicted and of having her old automobile repossessed. No car, no job.

Desperate, without family or friends in the area, she had turned to two national "pay day loan" companies.

The Methodist Justice Ministry monthly pays past-due rent for clients like Louise and her two children—if, that is, the landlord will not take our money and then evict the family anyway. We use money from contributions to pay rent and utilities to keep families from eviction and

"Even though I am here on time to pay it off in full?"

"You aren't here with cash. The contract says we are allowed to insist upon payment by cash. And you shouldn't have waited until the last second."

"How are people who need your loans in the first place supposed to come up with that kind of cash? The only place they can go for that amount of cash in a lump is here or a place like here."

"We make all this clear to them when we give them the money."

At this point, I had about 35 minutes to come up with $734.00 in cash. I got some help from the internet, sped to a bank that was fortunately only 12 blocks away, and got the $734.00 in cash.

I arrived back at the store. I tendered the $734.00 cash in the full amount.

"Our computer system is still down. I can't take the money."

"Why does the computer need to be up for you to accept cash? You told me 15 minutes ago that I should go get cash."

"I didn't say that I could accept cash without the computer being up. How I am supposed to know how much is owed without the computer?"

"You told me what was owed 15 minutes ago." And I showed her the note she had given me with the amount she had written on it. "You know how much is owed. And you can give me a handwritten receipt with the date and time of payment."

"I am not authorized to do that."

"So you are telling me that even though Louise is living up to the letter of her contract, through me, you are not authorized to accept this cash, and she will default on this loan as of a few minutes from now?"

"Are you always this rude?"

"Lady, I am just getting started."

I demanded the telephone number for her supervisor. I assume that she wanted me to be rude to someone else so she dialed the number for me and handed me the phone. I stood in front of this employee, who was trying to lock up, until I pleaded and threatened my way to a paralegal in their corporate, legal department. This legal assistant first told me that it was past 5 pm, so Louise was already automatically in default on the loan. This default had already been noted at 5 p.m. in their computer system.

"So, the computer is down when it comes to accepting a pay-off of a loan, but is still operating fine when it comes to automatically defaulting on the loan?"

CHAPTER 7

God's Justice and Mercy Proclaimed in the Parables of Jesus

THE DOMINANT NARRATIVE'S TEACHINGS about value, meaning, honor, happiness, and particularly about justice and mercy, are shallow failures. These teachings are like "chaff that the wind drives away" (Ps 1:4). They do not satisfy and they do not serve the individual or the community. These teachings have created a closed nation of individuals who are alone, fearful, suspicious, and at war with every person and every nation for things and pleasures that do not satisfy, ennoble, or save. This narrative has created and been created by a society of strangers and mere competitors, not a community of neighbors. The narrative has created and been created by an insular, entitled class of the super wealthy who lack effective empathy for working or poor people. This narrative is responsible for the increasing inequality, immobility, injustice and mercilessness of this culture.

The counter-narrative of Jesus is starkly and thoroughly in conflict with this dominant narrative. God's justice and mercy, as set forth in Our Lord's narrative, would satisfy, ennoble, save and create the true *shalom* that the dominant narrative manifestly does not. The plights of the women, children, and men that I describe in chapter 6 would be radically different if American Christians first admitted the depth of the conflict between the dominant narrative and the counter-narrative of Jesus, and chose to follow Jesus' way instead.

We must turn from an "abstract concept" of justice and mercy to the revelation of God's justice and God's mercy in Scripture, and *particularly in the parables of Jesus of Nazareth*. My answer to the true nature of God's justice and mercy lies in discerning what Jesus tells us in his parables that all are due.

13 And he said to them, "Do you not understand this parable? Then how will you understand all the parables? 14 The sower sows the word. 15 These are the ones on the path where the word is sown: when they hear, Satan immediately comes and takes away the word that is sown in them. 16 And these are the ones sown on rocky ground: when they hear the word, they immediately receive it with joy. 17 But they have no root, and endure only for a while; then, when trouble or persecution arises on account of the word, immediately they fall away. 18 And others are those sown among the thorns: these are the ones who hear the word, 19 but the cares of the world, and the lure of wealth, and the desire for other things come in and choke the word, and it yields nothing. 20 And these are the ones sown on the good soil: they hear the word and accept it and bear fruit, thirty and sixty and a hundredfold." (Mark 4:1–20)

We start with this parable of the sower because the entire thesis of this book of the interconnection of God's justice and mercy collapses if Jesus actually said what is attributed to him in verses 10–12.

There is something of a disconnect between the parable itself set forth at verses 3 through 9 and the privileged secret provided in explanation to the disciples at verses 10 through 20. For me, the explanation is inconsistent with the parable itself and is also internally inconsistent. And there is a terrible disconnect between the utter mercilessness of verses 10 through 12, and the mercy so incarnate in Jesus' other teachings and entire ministry. Did Jesus mercilessly keep secrets from the hungry, ill, crippled, suffering, and outcast members of the crowds that followed him, and upon whom he otherwise poured so much mercy? Apart from his initial response to the Syrophoenecian woman reported in Mark 7:24–30—a merciless response that he quickly corrected with a merciful healing—when did Jesus ever refuse to eat, touch, or heal anyone? Don't the parables illumine instead of conceal? Verses 10 through 12 are among the most doubtful, pernicious, and merciless in all of Hebrew and Greek Scripture.

If we consider the parable itself at verses 3 through 9 apart from the verses 13 through 20, we are left with a burning question: Why would a sower spread his precious seeds on a hard path, on rocky ground, and among thorns, as opposed to spreading them all on "good soil?" Is there anything at all surprising about what happened with the seeds sown on these hostile topographies?

But there are at least three problems to such an initial reaction as the understanding that Jesus intended.

First, such a reaction and interpretation does not allow for a surprise or a shocking twist in the parable. Surprises, shocks, and twists from the dominant narrative of the time were part and parcel of Jesus' parables. These surprises were some of the ways that he ensured that his parables would get under people's skins and change his listeners. Consider three of Jesus' best known parables. In the parable of the prodigal son, if the father had responded to the son's return by making him stay in the servant's quarters until the son proved himself and earned his way back into the family, would we remember this parable? Would it have challenged us and our usual way of thinking and reacting as it does? In the parable of the good Samaritan, wasn't it shocking to Jesus' listeners that it was the hated, alien enemy who was so merciful, and not the two professionally religious Jews? And in the parable of the workers in the vineyard, if the owner had paid the workers who were hired so late in the work day some fraction of a *denarius,* or if the owner had not made such a show to the longer laboring laborers of paying a full day's wage to the workers hired at the end of the work day, would this parable have gotten under the listeners' and the readers' skins as it has? So where is the surprise in the intended understanding of this parable of the sower that Jesus was merely telling us to be selective where we sow the word of God?

Second, wouldn't the listeners to the parable of the sower have known that Jesus sowed his word of mercy, his food, his healings, and indeed himself everywhere to everyone, no matter the ground? Wasn't this the crux of the controversy between Jesus and the religious insiders? In fact, didn't the Pharisees complain that he was sowing almost all of his seed in the most unsuitable places among the least-deserving people? Weren't the Pharisees and the scribes objecting that Jesus was wasting his words on sinners—the violators of Torah, the unclean, the impure, and the traitorous tax collectors? So was Jesus responding in this parable of the sower by telling his disciples and followers not to waste their time and their seed planting among Pharisees and the leaders of the synagogue, the Romans, and the wealthy because the planting would prove fruitless? But is this consistent with Jesus' other actions and teachings? How many stories are there in the gospels of him eating with, teaching, and being merciful to Pharisees, scribes, leaders of the synagogue, the wealthy, and even Romans and their collaborators the tax collectors? Jesus was indeed a sower like the sower in the parable, spreading his word of God's mercy

than the setting of the ministry of Jesus. The call of Isaiah was radically different than the call of Jesus. When Isaiah prophesied, the LORD had firmly decided to punish the people of Israel for their violation of Torah, for their worship of other gods and for the exploitation by the wealthy of the poor. The LORD charged the prophet Isaiah to speak a word of judgment and eminent punishment to the people, but not in a way that would cause them to actually repent and avoid the punishment. Part of Isaiah's call was to "[m]ake the mind of this people dull, and stop their ears, and shut their eyes so that they may not look with their eyes and listen with their ears and comprehend with their minds and turn and be healed" (Isa 6:10). But Jesus came for the absolutely opposite purpose of calling and persuading God's people to turn and repent, saying, "The time is fulfilled, and the kingdom of God has come near; repent, and trust in the good news" (Mark 1:14–15).

Jesus' stated purpose in Mark 4:11 of using parables to ensure that his words *not* bear fruit with outsiders is inconsistent with the abundance of the harvest described at verse 20. In verses 10 and 11, Jesus allegedly describes his use of parables as an intended impediment to the flourishing of the seed. But in the explanation at verses 13 through 20, he describes "Satan," "trouble or persecution," and "cares of the world, the lure of wealth, and the desire for other things" as the impediments. So verses 10 through 12 are inconsistent with verses 13 through 20. And verses 10 through 12 are inconsistent with the parable itself, unless we are to count Jesus' use of parables as the thorns that choke the word of the good news.

The clear purpose and success of Jesus' use of parables was to grow the kingdom of God, to plant mercifully a growing seed of understanding, influence, justice and mercy in people's hearts, and not to hide mercilessly the kingdom, its presence, its further coming, and its nature from people.

This pernicious explanation of Jesus' use of parables—that the use was to hide and obscure—is radically inconsistent with his teachings. "But strive first for the kingdom of God and his righteousness . . ." (Matt 6:33). "So I say to you, Ask and it will be given you; search and you will find, knock and the door will be opened for you. For everyone who asks receives, and everyone who searches finds, and for everyone who knocks, the door will be opened. Is there anyone among you who, if your child asks for a fish, will give a snake instead of a fish? Or if the child asks for an egg, will give a scorpion? If you then, who are evil, know how to give good gifts to your children, how much more will the heavenly Father

reading from what we call Isaiah 61 in his home synagogue in Nazareth (Luke 4:18–19), he told the "crowds" who wanted "to prevent him from leaving them" that "I must proclaim the good news of the kingdom of God to the other cities also; for I was sent for this purpose" (Luke 4:42–43). Intermingled with healings, he continued to spread this good news. He taught while "Pharisees and teachers of the law . . . from every village of Galilee and Judea and from Jerusalem" listened to him (Luke 5:17). He preached his Sermon on the Plain (Luke 6:20–49), to "a great crowd of his disciples and a great multitude of people from all Judea, Jerusalem, and the coast of Tyre and Sidon . . . who had come to hear him" (Luke 6:17–18). Part of that sermon was: "Why do you call me 'Lord, Lord,' and not do what I tell you?" (Luke 6:46). "[Be] someone . . . who comes to me, hears my words, and acts on them" (Luke 6:4). Thereafter, Jesus healed the slave of a Roman centurion (Luke 7:1–10), and then raised from the dead a poor widow's only son (Luke 7:11–15), causing the word that he was a "great prophet" to spread "throughout Judea and all the surrounding country" (Luke 7:16–17). Later he ate with a Pharisee in his home, and welcomed and defended a "woman of the city, who was a sinner" who intruded into the dinner to minister to him (Luke 7:36–50). "Soon afterwards he went on through the cities and villages, proclaiming and bringing the good news of the kingdom of God" (Luke 8:1). The twelve disciples and many women were with him (Luke 8:1–3). Then, when another "great crowd gathered" (Luke 8:4), he told the parable of the sower. And just after Jesus allegedly claimed that he taught in parables to hide secrets from outsiders, Jesus exhorted his followers to put their light on a lampstand that all may see, not hide their light under a jar or a bed (Luke 8:16). Then, when his family came to fetch him home, Jesus said, "My mother and brothers are those who hear the word of God and do it" (Luke 8:21).

Does this sound like Jesus was trying to hide "the secrets of the kingdom of God" (Luke 8:10) from the crowds of people who came to hear him? How would using parables to hide the truth of the kingdom of God be "good news"? Why would Jesus teach people to "come to me and hear my words and act on them" and then hide the meaning of his calls to action? Why would Jesus teach that those "who hear the word of God and do it" are his family, and then hide from people what that word meant and required? Why would people flock great distances from everywhere to hear the words of a man who taught hidden truths in stories that only a few insiders could understand? When everything that Jesus did and

attraction or power for them. Their hearts were like the path on which some of the seed fell. The response of the hearts of other listeners was at first receptive. But as the challenge of living out Jesus' proclamation of the kingdom grew evidently more challenging, the word died in them. They lacked the endurance and the courage to persevere. So their hearts are likened to rocks and thorns. But the hearts of others received the word and were changed by it into productive soil, so the word grew and flourished in their lives. "Let everyone who has ears to hear listen!" is a plea to listen and become "good soil," rather than hard path, rock or thorns. On this basis, when the word flourished and was productive, the listeners were due credit for the growth. And when the word died, it was because the listeners were due blame and even condemnation.

The explanation set forth in verses 13 through 20 turns the parable on its head. In the original, unexplained parable, it is hardly surprising what happened to these seeds—which seeds took root, thrived, and flourished and which seeds did not. It is a tortured explanation to make the persons on whom the seeds fell responsible for their flourishing or failing and not the sower who chose to sow on good and on inhospitable ground.

The key for me is in the parable itself, not in the appended explanation. The sower spreads his word to everyone in every setting, to the rich in settings of comfort and privilege, to the poor in settings of want and exclusion, and to everyone between. And the sower does so knowing that the word was much, much less likely to grow and flourish on some ground than the other. *But he sows everywhere to everyone anyway.*

As I read the parable itself, Jesus led the great, listening crowd to understand that the sower represented Jesus himself and that the seed was his word of the arriving kingdom of God's mercy. He described realistically the different way that his listeners could and would likely respond to the word, based upon their histories, families, economic situations, and social locations. *But Jesus, in his mercy, still sowed his word to everyone, everywhere.* He did not preach his word of mercy only to those whom he judged were due to hear it. He did not withhold it from sinners among the poor and the wealthy whom many believed were not deserving of mercy. He did not proclaim it only in a gathering of people allowed in after his disciples had screened and deemed them worthy or likely to respond productively. He did not proclaim it only among the Pharisees or the righteous few who claimed to live by every requirement of Torah, nor did he exclude those from his sowing. He did not proclaim

would expect, because this was so in conflict with the dominant narrative of Jesus' time, symbolized by the foolish farming practice of such sowing. This is also deeply in conflict with the same dominant narrative of our time—a narrative that dictates that people must earn our mercy before we are merciful, and that our mercy must be due to them based upon their actions, their capacity for reciprocity, their relationship to us, or the likelihood that our mercy will bear fruit by causing them to fix their lives as we want them fixed. In this parable, Jesus is saying to you and me, "Sow mercy to everyone, without first assessing who is and is not likely to respond in the way you want, and without assessing who you judge to be due your mercy."

But the Methodist Justice Ministry and I do not act faithfully in light of this parable. We receive 20 to 25 new requests for free legal representation and help each week. We screen closely those who request our help. We have limited resources, and we are looking for the worst cases and the people who will benefit the most from our help. But one criterion we work by is not to take the case of an abused woman whom we can predict based upon hard experience is likely to return to her abuser. We make this assessment based upon a variety of factors, but the one we rely upon the most is whether the potential client has previously and repeatedly left her abuser but then returned to him. From working in this ministry, we hope that we have a good appreciation for why a woman returns, often with children, to her abuser's home. Often the reason is financial—because she cannot provide for herself and her children alone. Often it is because the psychological abuse she has endured has sapped her of her confidence, energy, and hope. Often it is because her abuser has kept her completely dependent upon him, and unable to make her own way. These are among the reasons why we provide free professional counseling and financial support to our clients.

But in assessing our screening practice in the light of this parable of the sower, I doubt that we are being faithful to the life and teaching of Jesus, who sowed his seeds of mercy everywhere and on everyone all the time. We don't take certain cases because we don't want to "waste" our seeds and because we want the twelve judges we practice before to rely upon our bringing only "good" cases to them. But an abused woman who has previously escaped and then returned to her abuser and then has escaped again is at least as much in need of our active mercy as one who is leaving an abuser for the first time. So perhaps we should just sow our seed and let Jesus determine what fruit it will bear. When Jesus says,

born. That child would have every reason to be bitter and angry. How hospitable could that ground be to Jesus' seeds of mercy?

But the response of people to Jesus' seeds of mercy can still prove something of a mystery. People do break free of the ground of their birth and of their present. Some children from wealthy families who are exposed to Jesus seeds of mercy do choose lives of service and modest comforts, as opposed to self-centered pursuit of stuff and transient experiences. The seed does sometimes transform the ground. It's a mystery which children from the thorny ground of wealth will choose the way of mercy. And some children from the ghetto or from rural poverty, raised on ground of hopelessness, do respond to the hard bitterness of their past with lives of hope and service. Some who are able to escape their poverty return to help the people left behind. It is a mystery which children will do this. Children from the same parents in any ground can have radically different reactions to the word of mercy and the ground in which they were born and reared.

**

The Woman of the City and the Parable of the Two Debtors

36 One of the Pharisees asked Jesus to eat with him, and he went into the Pharisee's house and reclined at the table, 37 And the sort of woman in the city who was a wicked sinner, having learned that he was eating in the Pharisee's house, brought an alabaster jar of ointment. 38 She stood behind him at his feet, weeping, and began to bathe his feet with her tears and to dry them with her hair. Then she continued kissing his feet and anointing them with the ointment. 39 Now when the Pharisee who had invited him saw it, he said to himself, "If this man were a prophet, he would have known who and what kind of woman this is who is touching him—that she is a sinner." 40 Jesus spoke up and said to him, "Simon, I have something to say to you." "Teacher," he replied, "Speak." 41 "A certain creditor had two debtors; one owed five hundred denarii, and the other fifty. 42 When they could not pay, he canceled the debts for both of them. Now which of them will love him more?" 43 Simon answered, "I suppose the one for whom he canceled the greater debt." And Jesus said to him, "You have judged rightly." 44 Then turning toward the woman, he said to Simon, "Do you see this woman? I entered your house; you gave me no water for my

and so much else. Her trust, inspired by Jesus, "made her whole," just as the counter-narrative of Jesus seeks to create a world in which the poor and outcast of our time will be saved from the contempt of others and their own self-contempt learned from the dominant narrative of our time.

"Do you see this woman?" Jesus asks the Pharisee at verse 44. No, he does not. He does not see *her*. He sees only one of *them*. This unnamed woman could have been divorced, or widowed, or the daughter of an outcast. She could have been the daughter of a woman who was divorced and expelled by her husband, who then had to suffer in poverty and ostracism her entire life. She could have been born outside of marriage. Or her sin could have been violation of the purity laws of Torah, her failure to sacrifice or be cleansed after her monthly period, her eating of unclean foods in her poverty, or some sexual sins. The Pharisee is indiscriminate. A sinner is a sinner. She failed to perform the "thou shalts" and violated the "thou shalt nots." So he did not see *her*.

The Pharisee judges that Jesus is not a prophet. It was a given of that time that a prophet can see into the heart. The irony in the story is that Jesus could and did see into the heart of the woman and of the Pharisee. The Pharisee who cannot see thinks that he can.

This parable is about the interaction of God's justice and mercy. The Pharisee judges that the woman and Jesus are not due his mercy. He does not welcome the woman as a fellow child of God, as he did not welcome Jesus as an honored guest. His treatment of both shows he does not believe that they are due his mercy. He simply judges and condemns the woman as a sinner. And he judges and condemns Jesus for not judging and treating the woman as a sinner. According to the dominant narrative controlling the Pharisee, Jesus should have shared the Pharisee's judgement that the woman was not due to be so familiar with Jesus, to share his space, to touch him or to be merciful to him. In affording Jesus and the woman no mercy, the Pharisee renders onto them less than each of them are due under Jesus' and God's counter-narrative.

A decision we are called to make about this parable is who does the greater sinner of the parable represent—the woman of the city or the Pharisee?

The Pharisee probably heard the parable and concluded that it did not apply to him at all. If he recognized that one of the sinners in the parable represented him, he would have concluded that his sin was of course much less than the woman's. He would have concluded that he was in the position of the debtor whose debt was one tenth of the other debtor's. But

aback by the question, for he does not see that the purpose of forgiveness is to inspire love ("I suppose . . ." v. 43). Then Jesus says of the woman, "her sins, which were many, have been forgiven; *hence* she has shown great love" *(v. 47)*.

Why did Jesus represent this woman in his parable as a debtor who "could not pay" her debts, whether they were greater or lesser than the Pharisee's? Given the connection that Jesus makes in the parable between forgiveness of debt and the capability to love, this is the same as asking why she "could not love" until she was forgiven. Was it because her life had been so hard and unjust, because she had been so condemned and shunned? Was it because she did not trust herself and so was merciless to herself? This capacity to be merciful to herself was given back to her by Jesus' preaching, forgiveness, inclusion, and trust in her. She was freed to love by his mercy, and this merciful love poured back out of her in gratitude for the one who had saved her.

Why was it that the Pharisee is represented in the parable by a debtor who also "could not pay" his debts? This is also the same as asking why he "could not love." He could not love because he was trapped in a dominant narrative that devalued mercy and that made hard judgments of who was and was not due mercy. Given that he was trapped in this way of thinking and being, and that he resisted being saved from it, he would likely never be able to "pay" his debts to God.

The love this parable is about is mercy. Mercy is active, giving, compassionate, outpouring, and sacrificial love—a love that does not ask who and who is not due mercy, and a love that asks only what form mercy should take for particular persons in specific situations. In the story, the Pharisee showed no mercy to the woman at all. He barely tolerated her presence at the meal and probably did so because it enabled him to illustrate his condemnation of Jesus' association with sinners, adding to the Pharisee's sense of superiority. And the Pharisee showed no mercy in the form of true welcome to Jesus. He gave Jesus the bare minimum of hospitality. In the Pharisee's eyes, Jesus was due no more than this minimum as a matter of justice.

In clear and intended contrast, the poor woman was as merciful to Jesus as was possible for her. By her actions, she declared that Jesus was due all the mercy that she could give him in adoration and support. Jesus was due the courage she displayed in entering a private home where she knew she was counted as less than nothing. By this, she risked physical ejection and public shaming. She showed that Jesus was due the

have taught and shown me so much about mercy and justice. The stories of some of them are in chapter 6.

According to the dominant narrative of Jesus' time and of ours, this poor woman was not due the mercy that Jesus gave her. She wasn't due being included or allowed into the Pharisee's house. She wasn't due being allowed to touch Jesus and minister to him. And under the dominant narrative of Jesus' time, Jesus wasn't due the mercy that the woman gave him. He was a poor, itinerant preacher and healer who seemed to be without income, who consistently violated the rules that determined who was deserving of being on the inside and who on the outside, who associated with the unclean and the immoral, who was a failure because he never accumulated any stuff, and who taught against the necessary basis for a functioning society. The dominant narratives of all times say that a necessary foundation of any functioning society is the distinctions that must be made among people who are and are not deserving of the society's goods and honor. But within the counter-narrative of Jesus, the necessary foundation of any covenantal community is for its people to be merciful to all. In the world being created by the counter-narrative of Jesus, what we are all justly due is mercy and to be made merciful. By Jesus' own mercy, example, and welcome of this "woman of the city," she had received the greatest mercy—to be made merciful. And this was the greatest mercy—to be made merciful—which the Pharisee refused.

**

The Parable of the Good Samaritan

25 Just then a lawyer stood up to test Jesus. "Teacher," he said, "what must I do to inherit eternal life?" 26 He said to him, "What is written in the law? What do you read there?" 27 He answered, "You shall love the Lord your God with all your heart, and with all your soul, and with all your strength, and with all your mind; and your neighbor as yourself." 28 And he said to him, "You have given the right answer; do this, and you will live."

29 But wanting to justify himself, he asked Jesus, "And who is my neighbor?" 30 Jesus replied, "A man was going down from Jerusalem to Jericho, and fell into the hands of robbers, who stripped him, beat him, and went away, leaving him half dead. 31 Now by chance a priest was going down that road; and when he saw him, he passed by on the other side. 32 So likewise a

The root of the colloquy between the legal expert and Jesus was the legal command set forth in Lev 19:17: "You shall love the neighbor as yourself." We who are captive to the dominant narrative miss that this love of the neighbor is a *legal command*. It is not like our dominant narrative's view of mercy—optional, occasional, and disfavored. This love is not a feeling or sentiment. "Love" in Scripture is always active mercy. It is not just feelings of compassion and empathy. "Love" in Scripture is acted out compassion and empathy. Here, Jesus links the command from Deut 6:5 to love God with every part of our being with the command from Leviticus to love the neighbor as deeply and actively as we love ourselves. Jesus teaches us here that the only *way* we love God completely is by loving the neighbor and ourselves deeply. These two passages from Torah are declaring that just as God is due my active, merciful love ("you *shall* love the Lord your God"), and just as I am due my own active, merciful love ("You *shall* love . . . yourself"), the neighbor is due the same active, merciful love from me ("you *shall* love your neighbor as yourself"). Again, these are legal commandments and so a matter of justice. The teaching of Jesus is that the legal reward for obeying this law about what God, I, and the neighbor are due is eternal life (v. 25). By implication, what one is due for failing this command is eternal death. Inheritance (v. 25) of anything is a matter regulated by law, so even the use of the word "inherit" associates this Scripture with law and thus justice.

Many have tried to cast the lawyer of this encounter in a bad light, interpreting "wanting to justify himself" as a self-centered attempt to justify his own restrictions on who is and is not due his love. I interpret this differently. The expert on Torah was in fact asking Jesus whom he was required to love to become truly just. I have been taught that in Jesus' time and setting there was a debate between two major rabbinical schools about whether the "neighbor" who was due active mercy under Lev 19:17 was any Jew or only a Jew who observed Torah thoroughly. The lawyer was asking Jesus where he stood on this.

Jesus' famous parable explodes the limitations taught by the dominant narrative of that time and of our time about who is "due" our mercy. When the setting and meaning of this parable are understood in this way, the brilliance and creativity of Jesus as a storyteller is even more awe inspiring.

Focus first on what Jesus tells us, and does not tell us, about the victim. Jesus does not say whether he is just a Jew or a just Jew who scrupulously obeys Torah. He doesn't even tell us if he is a Jew. He is described

bound by the same Torah—the same Lev 19:18. By his actions, he revealed his version of justice. He revealed that the neighbor due his mercy was anyone in need.

Arguably, the priest, the Levite, and the Samaritan all knew one additional fact about the man in need—that he was found in the land of the Jews. This would have made it likely that he was a Jew. This was not enough to cause the priest and the Levite to act mercifully and was not enough to dissuade the Samaritan. This reinforces that the person to whom mercy was due, in the eyes of the Samaritan, was any man in need of mercy, even a potential enemy.

The Samaritan was not merciful in a token or self-centered manner. Unlike the mercy shown by so many modern Christians, the Samaritan's love clearly was not acted out just to make the Samaritan feel good about himself or to achieve some moral status. The Samaritan's mercy extended to what was actually needed for the man to recover.

At the end of the parable, Jesus famously reverses the lawyer's question. The initiation of the legal discussion on the application of the law to love one's neighbor was the lawyer's question, "And who is my neighbor?" The implication of the question was that the person in need had to prove that he was within the requirements of being "deserving"—of being a neighbor—before being "due" any mercy. Jesus reversed the inquiry by asking who "proved to be the neighbor of the man in need?" Jesus placed the burden on the one encountering a man in need to be a neighbor, rather than demanding that the man in need satisfy the requirements of being a neighbor first.

How counter this narrative is to the dominant narratives of Torah, Jesus' time, and our time. This parable invalidates *any* judgments dividing those to whom mercy is due from me and those to whom mercy is not due from me. *Any* person whom I encounter in need of mercy is my neighbor and is due my mercy as a matter of justice. The only criterion that makes a person due mercy is his or her need for mercy. By this parable, Jesus allows for no consideration of whether the person in need could someday prove capable of helping us when we need mercy. Jesus allows no prudent consideration of self-interest by those called to act as neighbors. Jesus allows no limitation on the merciful action. Jesus allows no qualification or question about what foolishness on the person's part placed him in a position to be injured. Jesus teaches that the just obligations of all people to all other people are shaped by a universal,

neither toil nor spin; yet I tell you, even Solomon in all his glory was not clothed like one of these. 28 But if God so clothes the grass of the field, which is alive today and tomorrow is thrown into the oven, how much more will he clothe you—you of little faith! 29 And do not keep striving for what you are to eat and what you are to drink, and do not keep worrying. 30 For it is the nations of the world that strive after all these things, and your Father knows that you need them. 31 Instead, strive for his kingdom, and these things will be given to you as well.

32 Do not be afraid, little flock, for it is your Father's good pleasure to give you the kingdom. 33 Sell your possessions, and give alms. Make purses for yourselves that do not wear out, an unfailing treasure in heaven, where no thief comes near and no moth destroys. 34 For where your treasure is, there your heart will be also." (Luke 12:13–34)

Was the timing of the rich fool's death merely a random coincidence? If so, this parable is merely a wisdom teaching that we cannot depend on our accumulation of many things for security and long life. If so, the main teaching here is that we can die at any time, despite our best calculations and accumulations.

Or was the timing of the rich fool's death—just after he had completed his new barns and vowed to take his ease, eat, drink, and be merry with his accumulation—a judgment and punishment for his greed (v. 15)? Was his death due him from his totally selfish hoarding of the abundant produce of the land, for his claims that the land had produced for his use alone ("*my* crops" in verse 17; "*my* barns," "*my* grain," "*my* goods" in verse 18), and for his idolatry in claiming that even his soul belonged only to himself and not to God ("*my* soul" in verse 19)? And was the timing of his death also an act of God to cause all of this produce and these goods to be enjoyed by the needy of the community? ("And the things you have prepared, whose will they be?" in verse 20b.)

I hear this parable as a judgment and a punishment, which are both justice issues. The rich fool was intending to use these abundant goods only for himself. Within Jesus' counter-narrative, the poor were due the rich fool's mercy, and his failure to be abundantly merciful with his excess caused him to suffer the just punishment of a quick death. The abundance of these goods would support a lifestyle of luxury for many years. The man was due judgment and punishment merely for failing to share his huge excess, even if Jesus does not state that he obtained that excess through cheating the poor of their land, seizing the land when the poor

whether to be "rich for himself" or "rich for God," and begins in verse 17 when he considered within himself what he should do with his windfall of abundance.

This conversation would have been a debate about what the man's soul was due from the other aspects of himself—the man's fears and appetites—and what the total "he" was due from and for his soul. Having said this, Jesus' parable describes a one-sided debate, because "he" didn't allow his *psychē* to be heard. The aspect of himself where fear, worry, greed, appetite, desire for pleasure, and ambition for personal honor reside—the place where the fool lives in all of us—shut up and out the aspect of himself where trust, faith, empathy, generosity, justice, and mercy reside. What the man in his totality decided that "he" was due was to use this abundance only for himself so he could be certain that he could "take his ease, eat, drink, and be merry" for the rest of his days. This man did not render what was truly due to his own soul and his own total self.

This moment of possible, actual dialogue in the inner decision making is described in this parable. In that moment there was the possibility of the rich man deciding not to be a fool, deciding instead to be merciful with his excess to those in need in his community, and deciding to be rich toward God instead of toward his appetite and fear of not having enough for himself. This moment of possibility was in a space between verses 17 and 18—an instant when his *psychē* could have spoken out for mercy instead of selfishness, and for trust in God instead of hoarding out of fear. It could have been more than a moment's space in time, more than a moment's pause. But in this parable, the *psychē* is either silent or was shut out before she could express herself. Perhaps in this man, his *psychē* was very weak from lack of nurture and from the destructive effects of the dominant narrative of that time.

This man depended upon externals for his meaning, honor, and satisfaction, upon his accumulation and selfish enjoyment of the abundant harvest, and the ostentation of tearing down and building new barns. The dominant narrative of his time taught him that these externals were the only sources of such meaning, honor, and satisfaction. So he shut out the urges to justice and mercy that were present within his own soul, and failed to find the greater meaning, honor and satisfaction that come from these internals. He failed to be just and merciful to himself. This failure is where all injustice and mercilessness to others begins. He was like an addict who fears that he cannot find happiness from the resources that he has within himself, and that he must turn to drugs for happiness. This

about ourselves, our mortal lives, our things, and our status. Jesus teaches that the soul is due the self's not striving after these things. What is the soul due from the total self? The soul is due being allowed to grow in trust that God will provide what is truly needed. The soul is due the entire self's striving after God's kingdom (verse 31) over all else. The soul and the entire self are due being merciful.

What is God due? God is due that we place all of our energy in striving for the kingdom. God is due what our souls are due. God is due for us not to be distracted by other concerns. God is due for us to trust God rather than our appetites, fears, and accumulations. God is due for us to depend upon God's grace alone, rather than upon our own striving. God is due for us to use our possessions to be rich toward God through mercy to others in need, rather than to be rich toward ourselves through greed. In fact, the irony is that accumulating wealth for our own use is *not* being rich toward our souls. Being merciful is being rich to our souls. God is due for us to trust that being rich toward God through mercy to others is also being rich toward our own souls, and is the way to true life.

There is a fourth character present in this parable besides the man, his soul and God. It is the listening crowd. Luke 12:1, which is the beginning of this section of encounter and teaching, describes that the crowd gathered "by the thousands" to be taught, fed and healed by Jesus. We know from the gospels that the crowd following Jesus was largely comprised of those in great need and those considered by religious insiders as unclean "sinners." This parable of the rich fool was spoken in their hearing, though likely directed to the religious insiders who were also present. The rich man in the parable used his abundance as if the people in the crowd did not matter, much like the rich man did in Luke 16:19–31. The rich fool in this parable lived as if life were a contest in which all the characters were merely contestants. He did not live as if life were a covenant with God and with his neighbor. So he lived as if he was due whatever he could get and consume, and as if the members of the crowd were not due what they did not have. In short, he lived according to the dominant narrative of his time and of our time, not according to the counter-narrative of God.

The rich fool showed by his life that he believed he was due the consumption and use for his body alone of all that "his" land produced. And he behaved as if this was the sole meaning of life. He was already rich, and became even richer when his land produced abundantly. The abundance was so great that the multiple storage facilities that he already

kingdom, we will be given what we need. Luke 12:29–31 reads: "And do not keep striving for what you are to eat and what you are to drink, and do not keep worrying. For it is the nations of the world that strive after all these things, and your Father knows that you need them. Instead, strive for his kingdom, and these things will be given to you as well."

This is not just a startling affirmation because it is so counter to the dominant narrative of that time and our time. It is also startling because it is so challenging to trust like this as a practical matter. Jesus says here, "Do not worry and be distracted about material security and wealth, and do not be greedy . . . *because* God will provide what you need if you strive single-mindedly for the kingdom. You are free and able to render to all in need the mercy and generosity they are due—your neighbor, God, and even your own soul—*because* God will provide what you need if you strive for the kingdom."

Really? Is that the way it works in your neighborhood?

Why don't we trust God to decide what it is we truly need? Is it because we want to be the ones to decide what we need? (We think that we decide what we need, but, in fact, it is the dominant narrative that decides.) We don't trust God because we want the honor from winning the competition to take what the dominant narrative tells us we need and not to be given it with everyone else. The dominant narrative tells us that we will never have enough of what it dictates that we need. We do not trust God's counter-narrative that tells us what we truly need to make our lives satisfying and meaningful is no more than what we need to survive and be merciful.

Is it because our experience is that God will not give us the material things we need to live and be merciful? If we strive single-mindedly for the kingdom, will God then provide what we truly need? If we are not distracted from single-minded striving for the kingdom, if we do not fall into the worry and anxiety from the distraction of things and from transient pleasures, will God "give" us what we "need?" Have any of us tried this to be able to say whether it is true? Has the American church, cradled in the arms of the dominant narrative, shown or taught that this teaching can or should be followed?

Whether this teaching of Jesus, and the promise of God he communicates, are true depends upon (1) what we need, (2) what the kingdom does and would look like, and (3) how God gives. As to God "giving" our material needs to us, Jesus teaches us through both versions of the Lord's Prayer at Matthew 6:11 and Luke 11:3 to ask our Father to *"give"* us

who welcomed them to shelter and feed them. And in Luke 10:1–9, he is reported to have given the same instructions to the "seventy," including to depend upon those who welcomed them for their material needs. Jesus did not tell the twelve and then the seventy to take no bread, and no money to buy bread and pay for lodging, because God would make their material needs fall from the sky like the manna and quail in the wilderness story. He instead told them, in effect, to strive for the kingdom. If they did, then God would give them their bread and material needs through the mercy of generosity of the people in whose households they were welcomed in the power and presence of that kingdom, whose counter-narrative included the mercy of generosity.

Between the two stories of the twelve and the seventy quoted above, and just after the return of the twelve from their mission, Luke reports that Jesus brought about the feeding of thousands of hungry people (Luke 9:10–17). This feeding story is proclaimed in all four Gospels. Clearly, sharing food and making sure that all had enough of their material needs to live were and are essential parts of the kingdom of God. Part of this feeding story is symbolic of the Eucharist and the abundant availability of that holy bread and cup to everyone. But the telling verse to me in all three versions in the Synoptic Gospels, particularly when read in conjunction with the missions of the twelve and the seventy, is "You give them something to eat" at verse 13 of Luke's version. The followers of Jesus will receive the bread, shelter, and their other material necessities when they strive single-mindedly for the kingdom, because the community of the strivers after the kingdom will share material necessities with others. This is an essential part of the striving and of the kingdom itself. (See also, among many teachings, Luke 6:30a, 35c, 38; 9:1b; 10:6–9, 34–35; 14:13; 18:22; 19:8–10; and Matt 25:3–36.)

So when Jesus says at Luke 12:29–31 "[D]o not keep striving for what you are to eat and what you are to drink, and do not keep worrying . . . [Y]our Father knows that you need them. Instead, strive for his kingdom, and these things will be given to you as well," he simply and confidently means that striving for the kingdom includes receiving the material things we really need and sharing our excess so that others can live and share. Part of the striving for the kingdom is this merciful sharing. The way that God will "give" what we truly need to us will be through the growing kingdom and through the others who are faithfully striving for it. Within the growing kingdom, we will all give and receive the mercy we need to live and be merciful, and we will all limit ourselves to the

brothers or your relatives or rich neighbors, in case they may invite you in return, and you would be repaid. 13 But when you give a banquet, invite the poor, the crippled, the lame, and the blind. 14 And you will be blessed, because they cannot repay you, for you will be repaid at the resurrection of the righteous."

15 One of the dinner guests, on hearing this, said to him, "Blessed is anyone who will eat bread in the kingdom of God!" 16 Then Jesus said to him, "Someone gave a great dinner and invited many. 17 At the time for the dinner he sent his slave to say to those who had been invited, 'Come; for everything is ready now.' 18 But they all alike began to make excuses. The first said to him, 'I have bought a piece of land, and I must go out and see it; please accept my regrets.' 19 Another said, 'I have bought five yoke of oxen, and I am going to try them out; please accept my regrets.' 20 Another said, 'I have just been married, and therefore I cannot come.' 21 So the slave returned and reported this to his master. Then the owner of the house became angry and said to his slave, 'Go out at once into the streets and lanes of the town and bring in the poor, the crippled, the blind, and the lame.' 22 And the slave said, 'Sir, what you ordered has been done, and there is still room.' 23 Then the master said to the slave, 'Go out into the roads and lanes, and compel people to come in, so that my house may be filled. 24 For I tell you, none of those who were invited will taste my dinner.'" (Luke 14:1–24)

I understand this parable by starting with (1) the hopes and expectations of an end-time banquet inaugurating a new, messianic age, and (2) the verses preceding this parable that condemn the insider/outsider system of the dominant narrative of Jesus' day.

Verse 15 is for me a reference to the eschatological banquet, the promised banquet announcing the end of the age when the world is broken. That banquet was to be a great and joyous celebration of the arrival of the time when this world would be restored to its intended form by the intervention of God. Isaiah 25 was a source of this hope and expectation:

> 1 O LORD, you are my God;
>> I will exalt you, I will praise your name;
> for you have done wonderful things,
>> plans formed of old, faithful and sure . . .

> 6 On this mountain the LORD of hosts will make for all peoples

to be merciful. But within Jesus' counter-narrative, you are called to in-vite people solely out of mercy and those people who cannot reciprocate. Within this new narrative for the new age, the people of God are called to "[b]e merciful, just as your Father is merciful" (Luke 6:36). Jesus calls us to eliminate insider/outsider considerations and the reciprocal benefit calculation. Verse 11 is a clear condemnation of calculations of who is due and who is not due. According to the dominant narrative of that time, a man strived for social honor by proving that he was due more honor than others were due. Jesus' teaching is: "He who claims that he is due more honor than another is actually due less. And he who refrains from claiming that he is due honor is due the most honor in the new kingdom."

Picture the setting for this parable of the great feast as a Sabbath banquet hosted and attended mostly by insiders. Many are gathered in the courtyard of the home of this leader of the Pharisees, reclining at a low table. The Pharisees and their guests are "watching [Jesus] closely" (Luke 14:1). Jesus was invited so that they might witness, hear for them-selves, and have a basis for condemning his errors. Jesus was leading people astray, destroying the separation between the clean and holy, on the one hand, and the unclean and defiled on the other. He was making undue mercy primary, rather than obedience to the purity and holiness code in Torah. He was eating with sinners. What the Pharisees and their insiders did not see was that Jesus was eating with sinners at this meal with insiders.

Just as people were arriving, Jesus noticed that the guests were jockeying for the places of greatest honor at the table. Knowing why he had been included, Jesus himself started the debate about who is due the honor and admission into the "inside."

First, Jesus started the controversy by healing on the Sabbath a man with dropsy, an edema caused by an excess of fluid, perhaps caused by a kidney or a circulatory problem. The man happened to be present; there is no claim in the story that a Pharisee had invited him. Meals in that setting were often held in an uncovered courtyard, and passersby were able to stop and observe. What I read here is that Jesus saw this suffering man on the outside of the courtyard and brought him inside. He did this to confront the Pharisees about their priority of observing Torah Sab-bath rules over the call of the Torah and the prophets to be merciful. Because this man's condition was not one from which he could die if not addressed that very Sabbath day, the Pharisees contended that there

Jesus will not relent. Too much harm was being done by this domi-nant narrative. So, fourth, Jesus tells the parable of the great dinner about who is invited and who actually accepts the invitation to the banquet, to bring this guest and all in attendance up short. It was surely a fourth challenge to those who were so smug about being insiders.

A concern is whether it is *only after* the insiders are invited, ac-cept initially, and then refuse to come that the outsiders—"the poor, the crippled, the blind, and the lame"—are invited. But I finally understand that Jesus told the parable in this way to heighten the criticism of the failure of the so-called insiders to understand and respond to God's true will. "Have it your way," says Jesus to the insiders. "You had priority. You were invited first. But you failed to appreciate the value and meaning of your invitation. You are too comfortable and smug. The world is all right with you just as it is. You aren't hungry enough for the coming of the kingdom to abandon your hierarchies to come to God's feast where the world will be changed radically. So God turns to people who are hungry and humble, and who will truly appreciate the value of the arrival of the kingdom and the radical change it brings and requires."

In the parable, the "someone" is representative of God. The story also assumes that the three persons described in verses 18, 19, and 20 had originally accepted the initial invitation, and that there was a delay between the invitation, the acceptance, and the start of the "great din-ner." Then those three offered weak excuses for backing out, showing that routine activities of benefit to them were more important than the great changes coming with the new age.

At least two of the excuses are weak. The first two even seem false. Who waits until after he has purchased land to inspect it? Who purchases five yoke of oxen and only then test drives them, so to speak? These ex-cuses are flimsy attempts to get out of a previous acceptance, because they decided they did not want the changes that will come with the banquet.

There is a parallel between the excuses of the three invitees and the Pharisees' condemnation of Jesus healing the man with dropsy. The Phar-isees claimed that the healing on the Sabbath was in violation of Torah because there was nothing urgent in the man's condition that required healing that day. In the same way, there was nothing urgent requiring the man to go on the day of the banquet to see the land he had already purchased, or requiring the man to go that day to try out the yoke of oxen he already owned, or requiring the man to be with his wife that day when he would enjoy a lifetime with her. Priority is the major lesson of

Pharisees refused the invitation because the world was much more than alright with them. The poor, crippled, lame, and blind flooded in because for them the world was broken.

There is an interesting claim within the narrative of this parable as to why God invited the needy outsiders of the town and then of the country after the insiders backed out. Why did God not simply throw the food away? "'Sir, what you ordered has been done, and *there is still room*" (v. 22). "Then the master said to the slave, 'Go out into the roads and lanes and compel people to come in, so that my house may be filled" (v. 23). In the narrative, God felt a powerful urge to feed, to inaugurate the new age, to be merciful and to bring *all* people together. And no failure by the most privileged but unappreciative of people could thwart the feast giver's will.

As to the "compelling" ordered in verse 23, I view this not as force of violence but of the compelling power of the gospel—the good news of a transformed world for all people and particularly the suffering. "Compel" them refers to the urgency and attraction of the invitation.

Luke 1:50–53 is a precursor to this parable: "His mercy is for those who fear him from generation to generation. He has shown strength with his arm; he has scattered the proud in the thoughts of their hearts. He has brought down the powerful from their thrones, and lifted up the lowly; *he has filled the hungry with good things, and sent the rich away empty.*"

Is this parable also an expansion of the parable at Luke 14:28–31?

> 28 For which of you, intending to build a tower, does not first sit down and estimate the cost, to see whether he has enough to complete it? 29 Otherwise, when he has laid a foundation and is not able to finish, all who see it will begin to ridicule him, 30 saying, "This fellow began to build and was not able to finish." 31 Or what king, going out to wage war against another king, will not sit down first and consider whether he is able with ten thousand to oppose the one who comes against him with twenty thousand?

In other words, do not initially accept Jesus' invitation to join with him on his way without "first" considering whether you are willing to give up all else. Do not hypocritically say that you will come to his banquet but then balk when all that you must give up becomes real to you. Each one who refused to come had offers and opportunities that they did not turn down even though they had already accepted the banquet invitation. The banquet was not that important to them. But to the poor and the

dominant narrative. Under Jesus' narrative they receive it only because they need it—the welcome, inclusion, and the food. They are all Lazarus. But in the end some have to be compelled to come in because they have internalized the dominant narrative and would feel ashamed or embarrassed to come.

In the setting of Jesus' telling of this parable, was it also about who will accept the mercy and who will not? Is the paradox that those who believe they are due the mercy do not accept the mercy, while those who are told by the dominant narrative that they did not deserve it accept it eagerly? The rich do not appreciate that this offer of mercy is much, much more valuable than any of the goods and interests that motivated the excuse-giver not to come. Salvation from the shroud of death in all its forms is worth giving up everything else.

There is an additional way to interpret this parable. Maybe the dominant narrative of the time prevented the three original invitees from believing that a poor, itinerant rabbi who associated with the unclean and the sinner was the one described in Isa 11:1–9. Maybe the three original invitees just couldn't bring themselves to believe that the end-time when God would fix the world was beginning with this one Jesus and his banquet. Maybe they had experienced too much of the realities and struggles of real life to believe that a time would ever come when:

> The wolf shall live with the lamb,
>> the leopard shall lie down with the kid,
> the calf and the lion and the fatling together,
>> and a little child shall lead them.
> The cow and the bear shall graze,
>> their young shall lie down together;
> and the lion shall eat straw like the ox.
>> The nursing child shall play over the hole of the asp,
> and the weaned child shall put its hand on the adder's den.
>> They will not hurt or destroy on all my holy mountain;
> for the earth will be full of the knowledge of the LORD
>> as the waters cover the sea. (Isa 11:6–9)

And maybe they believed that the world was so stuck in its ways that only a warrior at the head an army empowered by the Lord of Hosts could truly hold the wolves, the leopards, the bears, the lions, the asps, and the adders at bay. Maybe they viewed Jesus and his promises not

person hears the call of Jesus to drop all that and to come to the Great Dinner.

Imagine that the second person of the parable was a woman working on implementation of a plan to house all the homeless in a large city and to treat all of the causes of their homelessness. Years upon years of her efforts go without the numbers of chronically ill and disabled homeless being reduced. Then she hears the call of Jesus to drop it all and to come to the Great Dinner in which God will be the agent to house and treat the homeless.

Imagine that the third person of the parable had given up working and hoping and had just retired to the pleasures of family. Imagine that this third person was formerly the first person who fought against torture or the second person who was battling homelessness and its causes. And now that person has received the blessings of love in a marriage. But then he or she hears the same call of Jesus to leave the family and come to the Great Dinner.

What would that call mean today in these contexts? We know today that the Final Fix of God has not come as predicted and heralded by Jesus. So the call now is to do what . . . without the belief in the imminence of the Fix? To stop asking courts to prevent inhumane interrogation of suspected terrorists? Surely not. To quit trying to house and treat the homeless? Surely not. To quit strengthening the family? Most certainly not.

As many have said and written, including Albert Schweitzer in his *Search for the Historical Jesus,* Jesus' teachings look considerably different, and their application even more challenging, if we remove them from the context of belief in an *imminent* Day of the Lord.

But in the modern context, without this hope that God will soon or even ever bring the Final Fix, can or should we persevere in Jesus' way of extravagant mercy? Can we persevere in the way of Jesus without a powerful hope that God will someday bundle all our efforts with God's own into a Fix? Or do we just persevere through crisis after crisis after crisis until we are burned out? If we were to be offered a Final Fix now, if we would just leave everything we do and leave everything to God, would we go? Or would we hedge our bets and keep back a little means of working in a still broken world for ourselves, our families, and the suffering?

Doesn't the church's accommodation to the dominant narrative have at its foundation a doubt in the coming of this final, end-time fix by God of a broken world?

calm fear and defeat want, missed Jesus' point that the rules were chang-
ing radically with the arrival of the kingdom. Even a concern with family
and a priority on family relationships was being eclipsed by the call of
the arriving kingdom that was represented by the invitation to the Great
Dinner (see Luke 8:19–21; 9:23–25, 59–62; 12:22–34; 14:25–33; and
18:26–33).

It is not Jesus' belief in an imminent apocalypse that most separates
the comfortable American church from him. What separates us most
from him is the intensity of Jesus' pain at the injustice and mercilessness of the human world and the dominant narrative of his time. Even
though the fully incarnate Jesus was mistaken about how fully or soon
the kingdom of God was to arrive to put things right, we are called to
share his pain at this brokenness, and to see the world as he did and does.
We are called to yearn as he did for a world that is born anew, and for the
coming of a kingdom in which loving and sacrificial mercy reigns—not
self-serving violence, avarice and mercilessness. In order for the eternal
Word to be incarnate, that Word had to be enfleshed in a particular body
in a particular place and time. In that place and time, the hope was wide-
spread for the imminence of the coming day of the LORD, represented by
a great banquet, in which the LORD would fix a broken world. But Jesus'
life, yearning, and teaching of justice and mercy is not bound to a particular time and place. So we are called to lean into a kingdom in which
justice and mercy reign, to live into it, to enflesh it now as best we can.

Even if the kingdom never finally comes, even if this out-of-whack
human creation is never put back into whack by God, even if all we can
do is to inject justice and mercy crisis by crisis into a world of injustice
and mercilessness, we will still be living a more joyful and satisfying life
than offered by any and all of the dominant narratives of the world. We
will still be living the hope, faith, and love of Jesus. And we will still feel
his mysterious presence in the acts of just mercy we carry out. We will
see his mysterious presence in the eyes of the people to whom we bring
Jesus' heart of just mercy.

**

The Parable of the Prodigal Son

11 Then Jesus said, "There was a man who had two sons. 12 The
younger of them said to his father, 'Father, give me the share of

This parable was, I am sure, scandalous in Jesus' time. And it is scandalous now if we understand it correctly. The retelling and the rehearing of this parable has reduced its impact upon us. This parable is completely about justice and mercy, about what we think we and the wrongdoer are due, and about what we think we and the wrongdoer are not due. The father in this parable is a particularly rich and complex figure. Unlike so many commentators and preachers, I do not believe that Jesus intends to present the father in a totally positive light. And unlike the burden of Christian preaching and commentary on this parable, I do not find anywhere that Jesus intended that we should see the father as a complete or satisfactory symbol for God. I do not believe that Jesus intended any of the characters in the parable to be models for our own just and merciful conduct. I believe instead that Jesus told this parable with the intention that those who heard it would be troubled enough to question the justice and mercy of the father and to consider the complexity and goals of the mercy and justice to which we are called.

The beginning of the parable is filled with injustice—of a son demanding what was not due him, and a father giving what was not due to the son, of a son treating the father in a merciless manner that the father was not due, and the father treating the son in a way that was not due him, that was not going to benefit him, and that was therefore not merciful.

The younger son was only due the property he demanded when his father died. Verse 12 makes this clear in the son's demand: "Father, give me the share of the property that *will* belong to me." The property, which amounted to one third of the father's estate, would justly belong to him only when his father died and not a moment earlier. But the younger son demands it now, as if his father were already dead to the son. He thus treats his father in a way that the father is not due, and he treats him mercilessly. *Thus the parable teaches that injustice and mercilessness are aspects of the same conduct.* That the behavior of the son was tantamount to a claim that the father was dead to him is also shown in the language of verses 12 and 30. The Greek of verse 12 translates literally, "So he divided to them his life." The Greek of verse 30 translates, "who has devoured your [the father's] life with prostitutes."

Not only did the young son initially demand property as if his father were dead, but he then abandoned the father to go to a "distant country." Rather than staying so that he could be of merciful help to which his

The end of verse 12 states that the father divided his property "between them." I have heard many preachers interpret "them" to refer to the younger son and the older son. Based upon common practice from that time, the father could have assigned day-to-day control of two thirds of his property to his older son while maintaining actual ownership in himself. The older son would only inherit full ownership when the father died.

But this is a problematic interpretation because the father still seems to have full ownership and control of property to give his returning younger son. Upon the prodigal's return, the older son objects that he has continued to work for his father "like a slave" and has always obeyed the father's command (verse 29) after the younger son had left with his portion of the divided property. Verse 29 also states that the father had failed to give the older son even a goat for a party. In verse 30, the older son states that the younger son had returned to "devour *your* property," meaning the property of the father's. If the father divided all of his property between his two sons, why did the father still have total control of this property, including the fatted calf, the fine robe, the rings, and the sandals he gave to his younger son upon his return? And why could the older son not use his own goat for a celebration with his friends?

My reading of this parable is either that the "them" of verse 12 refers to the younger son and the father, or that Jesus is saying that the older son did not accept the division of the property before the father's death, because this son was a just and merciful man. It may be a stretch, but I prefer this latter interpretation. The older brother recognized that he was not yet due this two thirds of the property, and that his father was not due to be treated as if he were already dead. So his objection to his father's forgiveness and immediate restoration of his younger brother is all the more understandable. Under this reading, it was Jesus' genius to make this older brother the representative of the dominant narrative of Jesus' time. To this older brother, the father's mercy to the younger brother was scandalously unjust, just as the father's initial giving away of a portion of his property was unjust. The younger brother was not due this mercy of forgiveness and welcome, because he had been unjust and merciless to the father.

Before his return, the younger son wasted the property in degrading and undisciplined living. He had lived as if he was due immediately whatever he wanted to have and do. He behaved faithfully to the dominant narrative of his and our time. But by this behavior, he had treated

In his outrage at the injustice in the ways he and his younger brother were being treated, the older brother treats the father in a way that the father is not due. In that time and place, fathers were due to be obeyed. The older son affirms this in verse 29. "I have never disobeyed your commands." But now he is refusing the father's plea to go in to the party in disobedience (verse 28).

But the father does not stand on his command and does not upbraid the older brother for being disobedient. Instead, he "pleads" (verse 28) with the older son. To do what? To act mercifully.

What does the father tell the older son that the younger son is due? He tells the older son that the younger son is due mercy, merely because of his need. In that sense, the younger son is like the man in need in the parable of the Good Samaritan, except that we know that the younger son's wrongdoing caused his need. So the sum of both parables is that the one in need is due mercy whether or not he is responsible for his plight.

And what does the father tell the older son that he is due? To allow himself to be merciful! Verse 32 is translated: "But we had to celebrate and rejoice . . . " Another good translation of the Greek is: "It is due (Greek *dei*) for us to make merry and rejoice." The father tries to help the older son to see and embrace this.

Again, this parable is scandalous. I believe that Jesus intended it to be so. We, like Jesus' listeners, should fear that excusing so easily the younger son's terrible injustice and mercilessness will only enable him to repeat these when he is no longer in need of mercy. The parable would be less scandalous to us if, say, the father had honored his younger son's request to be accepted back as nothing more than a hired hand, at least until the younger son had suffered a "just" consequence for what he had done, until he showed by his conduct that he had learned his lesson, and until he proved his repentance was genuine. The father's love was so overpowering that he himself lacked the will to treat his younger son with the justice he had requested. Instead, the father acted out not only unconditional love toward the younger son, he also acted out scandalously unconditional mercy. This was partly for the benefit of the older son, to teach him to be merciful. What Jesus teaches us again in this parable is that the justice we are each due is mercy and to be made merciful.

But the scandal of the parable remains. Isn't accountability sometimes merciful and just? Isn't holding someone justly accountable for their actions sometimes in their interest and thus merciful to them? Can the particular form of our merciful actions be conditional while our love

let them back into the home. Sometimes these men have actually quoted Jesus to their abused women that they are required to forgive and take them back. When the woman takes the abuser back, the pattern repeats itself. We try to persuade the woman that taking the man back is certainly not merciful or just to her children or to herself. And we try to convince her that taking him back is also not just or merciful to the man, because it does not move him to actually repent, change his life, and become the just and merciful human being he should become.

So does the command of verse 4 mean that just because a wrong-doer "says" he repents we are required to forgive and restore him to the same relationship? After all, the father in the parable of the prodigal son did not just forgive his son. He restored him immediately to his former relationship with the robe, the rings, and the fatted calf.

But verse 4 should be read in conjunction with verse 3. Together they are one teaching. Reading these two verses together as they should be, forgiveness is not commanded merely after the wrongdoer "says" he repents. In verse 3, forgiveness must be given if there is "repentance." Repentance requires true change in deed as well as word, not just saying "I repent." So only if there is true change in heart, mind, and deed is forgiveness to be granted. Jesus' parables were often scandalous to have effect. That a wrongdoer could sin against the same person, be corrected for his mercilessness, actually repent in word and deed, and be forgiven—and then repeat that cycle six more times that very day—surely was not presented by Jesus as a realistic possibility. In this regard verse 3 is like its own parable.

Given Jesus' overall teachings and these two verses taken together, forgiveness is a species of God's mercy and justice. Why is forgiveness to be offered to the wrongdoer? For the moral purity of the one who is forgiving? No. Forgiveness is to be offered to benefit the wrongdoer by inspiring him to act in a mercifully loving manner (see Luke 7:47). So when someone acts mercilessly, he is to be corrected (v. 3). Why? So the one correcting can be righteous? No. So that the wrongdoer can become the merciful and just person he should be. If he merely says he repents but does not actually "bear fruit worthy of repentance" (Luke 3:8), forgiveness is not to be offered. Why not? Again, because it would not benefit and thus be a mercy to the wrongdoer.

Forgiveness can take many forms and progress through many stages, depending on what is merciful and just for all involved, including the wrongdoer. A wrongdoer can be forgiven but still not be restored

not listen to Moses and the prophets, neither will they be convinced even if someone rises from the dead." (Luke 16:19–31)

The rich man, who would have been the recipient of so much regard and honor within the world created by the dominant narrative of his day and whose name would have been well known by everyone in his community, goes unnamed in the world of the counter-narrative of this parable. Over the Christian centuries of preaching this parable, the anonymity of this rich man has evidently been so unsettling to preachers formed by the dominant narrative of their own times that they have given the rich man a name, thus obscuring some of the genius and intent of this parable. They utterly missed the point of Jesus' naming the poor man but not the rich one. So the preachers have named the rich man *Dives*, with a capital "D," from the Latin for "rich man" in the Vulgate Bible.

Under the dominant narrative of Jesus' time, the homeless beggar named Lazarus by Jesus would have been ignored, blamed for his own suffering, and avoided, just as homeless men and women are avoided under our own dominant narrative. The only attention the poor man would have received would have been held noses, avoidance, derision, and condemnation. People would have averted their eyes from this man, refusing to look him in the face for fear of being confronted by his torment and of being asked for alms. His sores would have caused him to be shunned all the more. In the world of that dominant narrative, no one would have cared to learn his name.

So Jesus is making a sharp point in giving him a name. And not just any name. Jesus called him "Lazarus" from the Greek form of the Hebrew *Eleazar,* meaning "God helps." The irony of this counter-narrative could not be thicker. The one whom the dominant narrative assumed to have been blessed by God through wealth, honor, health, and ease is unnamed and eventually condemned to an eternity of torment worse even than Lazarus' suffering on earth. The one whom the dominant narrative of Jesus' time assumed was being punished by God through homelessness, sores, and lameness was named "God helps." And in the parable, God eventually did.

Jesus tells us that the rich man was so rich that he was capable of abundant mercy to Lazarus without sacrificing his own comfort. And there is no claim that the rich man was due his riches by his hard work. Jesus tells us instead that he was rich because his father was rich, an accident of the unnamed rich man's birth. Just before he died, the rich man

failed to be merciful to another man who was not a member of his family or his close circle of friends. According to the dominant narrative of our time, there is generally no legal duty enforceable by punishment to come to the aid of anyone who is not in a very close relationship of dependence and vulnerability to us. For instance, the duty of a parent to a child to provide necessities is enforceable by criminal and family law statute in every jurisdiction in the United States. Within our dominant system, there are other voluntary relationships of dependence and vulnerability that can lead to a legally enforceable duty to be merciful by providing services and protecting the person. Examples are voluntary, mutual relationships between a doctor and patient, or between a lawyer and client, or within other fiduciary relationships. Even there, the punishments for failure to be merciful within those relationships vary in form and severity. But generally, as to every non-family member with whom I have not entered into such a voluntary relationship of dependence and vulnerability, my only just duty is not to harm them myself. Within the dominant narrative or our time, I have no just and punishable duty of rescue and provision. According to the dominant narrative of our time, if I were to provide for a suffering beggar at my gate, it would be a voluntary act of mercy on my part, not an act of justice due from me to the beggar.

Likewise, within the dominant narrative in which Jesus told this parable, the rich man and Lazarus were not family and had no voluntary relationship. Yet when the rich man died, he was sent to hell just for failing to be merciful to Lazarus.

Within the story world of this parable, the "Pharisees, who were lovers of money" (v. 14), did not accept that a man would be sent to hell for failing to be merciful to someone with whom they had no such relationship. The dominant narrative of that time was that a man could justly "love" his own money—which is to say, could justly spend 90 percent on himself and his own pleasure so long as he tithed. But Jesus' parable taught that God's counter-narrative was rooted in the Torah and the prophets, not the dominant narrative. And within God's counter-narrative, the rich man's punishment of hell was a just sentence for failing to obey Torah and the prophets to render the mercy that was due Lazarus within that counter-narrative. These legal teachings and commandments included:

> 4 There will, however, be no one in need among you, because the Lord is sure to bless you in the land that the Lord your God is giving you as a possession to occupy, 5 if only you will obey the LORD your God you by diligently observing this entire

If you remove the yoke from among you,

> the pointing of the finger, the speaking of evil,

10 if you offer your food to the hungry

> and satisfy the needs of the afflicted,

then your light shall rise in the darkness

> and your gloom be like the noonday.

11 The LORD will guide you continually,

> and satisfy your needs in parched places,

and make your bones strong;

> and you shall be like a watered garden,

like a spring of water,

> whose waters never fail. (Isa 58:2, 3, 6–11)

For me, Jesus' parable of Lazarus and the rich man resonates with this passage from Isaiah 58. The rich man failed to "share bread" with the hungry beggar and failed to bring this "homeless poor" man "into his home." Therefore, when the rich man calls from the "parched place" of hell, the LORD does not say, "Here I am." When the rich man was "parched" and asked only for Lazarus to bring water to drip on his tongue, the rich man was refused. The rich man failed to see to it that his servants brought to Lazarus the discards and crumbs from his table, which may be a reference to the Torah teachings not to glean to the edge of a field or harvest to the edge of a vineyard so that the poor may benefit from what is left (Lev 19:9–10).

The rich man did not claim to be wholly innocent when he asked for mercy from hell. He had evidently learned from his torment what he had not learned from Torah and the prophets before his death. Perhaps Jesus is saying that the rich man's first-ever experience of suffering made him appreciate how Lazarus had suffered. A claim of innocence would surely have been accompanied by a request to be freed from hell and to join Abraham and Lazarus in heaven. Instead, the rich man's excuse for not opening his hand to Lazarus before they both died was that he did not know that the poor were due mercy as a matter of God's justice. He was saying that he did not know that a Jew would be punished with hell for failure to be justly merciful to the poor. So he prays that Lazarus be sent to his five brothers to "warn" them that mercy to the poor was a just requirement of Torah and that failure to be merciful would result in being denied mercy upon death.

parable of the sheep and the goats at Matthew 25:31–46. The goats who had failed to be merciful during their earthly lives were denied mercy at their deaths. These two parables have strong parallel features, including that the punished in both parables claimed ignorance as their defense. The rich man claimed weakly that he did not know that Torah and the prophets required him to be merciful to Lazarus, and the goats claimed strongly that they did not know that Jesus himself was with and within the suffering people whom the goats had failed to help.

Indeed, what could be more counter to the dominant narrative of our time? Under the power of that dominant narrative, in order to be successful and valuable we must dedicate our lives to our increasing accumulation of things and our own greater experience of pleasure. But God's counter-narrative given in Torah, the prophets, and Jesus' teachings warns that if we live by this dominant narrative, we had best enjoy our merciless lives to the hilt before we die because we will be tormented for our mercilessness for eternity afterward. This is the point of the punishments described by Jesus in his parables of the unjust man and Lazarus, of the rich fool, and of the sheep and the goats.

What more can we make of the "great chasm" that prevented Lazarus from being merciful to the rich man? The Greek is *chasma*, which means a "chasm, a gulf, a gap or a wide space." This is the only use of this word that I have found in the New Testament. One understanding is that the chasm or gap between Lazarus and the rich man after both had died was like the chasm or gulf of the rich man's closed gate before both had died. The implication, again, may be that the barrier after death was justly due the rich man because of the barrier he had enforced before his death. So the sinful barriers of indifference created by merciless humans before we die are made permanent by God against merciless human beings after we die. It is too late to repent after we die, this says.

I have a very difficult time giving into this interpretation, though it is clear. It presents God as utterly merciful before we die and relentlessly merciless afterward. It presents a double standard for God's behavior and ours. And it seems inconsistent with the life and other teachings of Jesus.

For me, the spine of Jesus' teachings is that all in need are due God's mercy from all of us as a matter of God's justice. Thus are justice and mercy aspects of the same, single Truth in the counter-narrative and kingdom of God. The dualism of the claimed conflict between justice and mercy of the dominant narrative is negated. If we make judgments about which needy person is or is not due our mercy, we are following the

heaven and hell. The rich man and his close circle had separated themselves from Lazarus and other homeless because of their claim that they were due God's mercies and blessings while Lazarus and the poor were not. The reason that Lazarus in heaven could not bring the small mercy of water to the rich man in hell was because "a great chasm" had been fixed between them. The dominant narrative—the rich man's claim that some are due mercy and some are not—had fixed the chasm, not God's mercilessness. The point of the parable was to inspire the self-righteous and comfortable to be merciful, not to describe the limits of our Father's mercy.

Likewise, nothing is said in the parable that Lazarus had received the greatest mercy of being "carried away to Abraham's side" because he had been merciful in his earthly life. The only reason given was that Lazarus was in need of mercy and had not received it in his physical life. In verses 25 and 29, Jesus has Abraham repeat in the hearing of the Pharisees the dominant narrative's claims about justice and mercy. To paraphrase, "In eternity, you receive your just deserts based upon what you did not do in life."

As to the rich man's other request that Lazarus be sent to his five brothers to tell them that mercy to the poor was an essential requirement of God's counter-justice, the reason that Lazarus would not be sent was: "If they will not listen to Moses and the prophets, neither will they be convinced even if someone rises from the dead" (verse 31). It would do no good to send Lazarus to them. But notice also the irony here. Was the reference to someone rising from the dead a reference to Jesus himself? Through this parable spoken by Jesus before he was crucified and raised, and through Luke's inclusion of the parable in his gospel, someone who was raised from the dead *was* warning everyone who would listen that mercy to the poor *is* an essential and just requirement of "Moses [Torah] and the prophets." Someone who had been raised from the dead *was* warning them of the just consequences of failing to be merciful within the world being created by God's counter-narrative. The parable, with so many others of Jesus' teachings, motivates and inspires us to be merciful in this life and to give hope to those who are in need of mercy. This parable itself communicates the warning to the "five brothers," who represent all of us.

I do not believe that the point is to actually describe what happens to us after death. I have always wondered why a merciful God would make a hard and fast decree that it is too late to repent of our mercilessness

God's suffering poor? How deep and wide and rich, how genuine would a mercy be, that could actually be produced by selfish ambition or fear? To inspire mercy, doesn't Jesus' brilliant parable of Lazarus and the rich man rely much more upon graphic description of the suffering of pitiful Lazarus outside the rich man's gate than upon the threat of hell?

> And at his gate was laid a beggar named Lazarus, covered with sores, who longed to eat what fell from the rich man's table. Even the dogs would come and lick his sores.

Even the description of the rich man in hell is intended by Jesus to inspire empathy and mercy:

> In Hell, where he was being tormented . . . "Father Abraham, have mercy on me, and send Lazarus to dip the tip of his finger in water and cool my tongue; for I am in agony in these flames."

The one thing the rich man and Lazarus had in common in the parable was their suffering and need for mercy, albeit at different stages of their lives and deaths. What God would be unmoved by such suffering after someone dies? The God described and incarnated by Jesus? The God revealed by and in Jesus' life and teachings? Perhaps another point of the "great chasm" of the parable is that a person who is unmoved to feelings of empathy and acts of mercy by the sight of extreme suffering will not be moved to such genuine empathy and mercy by the prospect of personal reward of bliss or the threat of terrible, personal punishment.

Put another way, was Ebenezer Scrooge's heartfelt and heartwarming repentance in Dickens classic *A Christmas Carol* mainly a result of the threat of eternal punishment? Or was it inspired and produced by Scrooge's witness and experience of the poverty and suffering of the Cratchit family and of the homeless poor under a London bridge? And did Dickens receive an inspiration for his work from verses 27–28 of this parable?

Why is one person deeply moved to empathy and mercy in the presence of another's suffering, while another person dismisses that suffering by blaming the sufferer for their plight? Why is empathy an overpowering experience in one person and merely a vague idea to another? Why do some people seek out people who are suffering and need mercy, while the majority of others avoid and deny the suffering? Some have claimed it has to do with the suffering that a person witnesses and experiences in life, particularly in childhood. Yet, siblings who experience the same

and few urges, and no sight of suffering, threat of punishment, or brilliant parable will increase them. Who really knows why? Who am I to judge?

So what is the point in *teaching* empathy and mercy? What is the point of proclaiming a counter-narrative of mercy to a culture controlled by a dominant narrative of mercilessness? What is the point of repeating Jesus' vivid parables about mercy and justice, suffering and need, accountability and forgiveness that serve mostly to emphasize that justice and mercy and their absence are matters of life and death to everyone? One point is to counter the merciless and unjust dominant narratives of every age and place, as well as the injustice and mercilessness that lurks in all of us. The point is to inspire the greatest possible just mercy and merciful justice in each and all of us. The point is to get the greatest number of Lazaruses in every age and place fed, dressed, sheltered, healed, and welcomed. The point of telling and repeating these parables is to shape and change the heart and soul of the human community in every age and place, and thus to shape every possible individual's goals, yearnings, and ethics. Jesus' parables are a major part of God's counter-narrative. Narratives shape the collective mind and the way of being and acting of entire peoples. They are a strong part of the "nurture" in the "nature or nurture" issue.

Among the greatest failures of the American church is our blindness to how deeply counter Jesus' narrative is to our dominant narrative, and our attempt to take turns living by each narrative—by the dominant narrative of narcissistic wealth during six and 23/24ths days a week, and the counter-narrative of just mercy and merciful justice for one hour of one day per week; by the counter-narrative during the Christmas and Lenten seasons and by the dominant narrative the rest of the year; by the counter-narrative in our relations with our family and friends but by the dominant narrative in every other arena of our lives and particularly in our economic, financial, and political lives.

A person who lacks the urge to be merciful is justly due . . . mercy— the mercy of understanding, acceptance, and encouragement to be more merciful.

A person who has this irresistible urge to be merciful is justly due mercy. For a person with this blessing, being merciful can bring almost a high. There can be not just joy but profound pleasure and *shalom* in helping someone who is in need. Being merciful can be an addiction for some of us. Persons who have this urge can be merciful to everyone but themselves and their families. Persons with this urge can burn out,

The key to this parable for me is the phrase in verse 7: "Will he [God] delay *long* in helping them?" (emphasis added). There, Jesus realistically recognizes that there has indeed been a delay. But he promises that God's delay was not due to God's lack of regard for them. He also promises that God's delay will not be long. Despite the delay, Jesus teaches his followers and listeners to be as persistent in pleading for justice and mercy from God as this widow was from the judge.

Regardless of the theological issue about God that is central to this parable, consider how very affirming and encouraging this parable would have been to those followers of Jesus who were as powerless and otherwise voiceless as this widow. This widow prevailed against her oppressors and against a merciless, unjust judge because of her courage and persistence!

The parable also affirms that God's justice and mercy are fused and that both are aspects of what is due even to the vulnerable and unprotected.

The main character is of course a widow. In Israel, the word "widow" was not used merely for a woman whose husband had died. While women could not inherit from their husband's estates, it was customary for a husband of any means to provide for the continued financial support of his wife after his death. If the deceased had done this in his life, the male who inherited the deceased husband's estate was obligated to provide for the widow. Even if a woman's husband died penniless, if she was protected and provided for by his or her family, she was not a "widow" in the sense of the Hebrew Scripture or this parable. A "widow" as used here was a woman whose husband had died without leaving her any financial support *and* who had no male to protect and advocate for her. A "widow" had no patron. She was like an orphan or an alien.

In the Hebrew Scripture, "widows, orphans and aliens" were a triad of persons who were representative of all those within Israel's covenantal community who were treated by the dominant narrative of that time as non-persons. They were treated as if they were due nothing from anyone. So Torah and the prophets contain many Scriptures specifically forbidding this oppression. (See, for example: Deut 24:17, 27:19; Isa 10:1–2; Jer 7:5–7; Zech 7:9–10; Mal 3:5.) These protections and admonitions were extraordinary, even unique, in the laws of the ancient Middle East. The inclusion of these protections for the poor and vulnerable reveals how different the people of YHWH were called to be, and how deeply counter the narrative of God was to the dominant narrative of the time. That there are many of these prohibitions and admonitions shows how often

> 23and repays vengeance on the nations;
> until he destroys the multitude of the insolent,
>   and breaks the scepters of the unrighteous;
> 24 until he repays mortals according to their deeds,
>   and the works of all according to their thoughts;
> 25 until he judges the case of his people
>   and makes them rejoice in his mercy.
> 26 His mercy is as welcome in time of distress
>   as clouds of rain in time of drought. (Sir 35:14–25)

In this parable, the widow had no one to protect or plead for her. Not one male would stand for her and protest the injustice that was being done to her. Not one man who was in the dominant inside would intercede even privately with the man who was exploiting this widow. She had no patron who would take her side. She was so alone and vulnerable that the only male to which she could turn was this merciless and unjust judge. But in refusing to call her case for consideration, he treated her like she was due no attention. She was of no account—a non-person. She was like a person in our time who had suffered a great injustice that did her great harm, but who could not find a lawyer because she could not pay, and who could not get a judge to hear her case because she did not know the proper procedure.

Perhaps this judge ignored the pleas of a widow because he had been bribed, or because the man who had treated her unjustly was a member of the same insider group as was the judge. The judge was showing partiality to this wrongdoer because they were friends and colleagues. Perhaps the wrongdoer was a merchant who had taken the widow's outer garment in pledge for food she desperately needed and was refusing to give it back. Perhaps the man was a landowner who had hired her to perform some task, and he was denying her some portion of what he agreed to pay her. Perhaps the man had taken something that belonged to her, like a goat or a donkey, claiming that she owed it to him, or that the animal had trespassed on his land, or that it was his not hers. Perhaps the landowner about whom she complains was the owner of a large amount of land in the region of this city. Suppose he habitually violated the protections afforded to the poor by Lev 19:9–10 by reaping to the very edges of his field, or gathering the gleanings of his harvest, or stripping his vineyards bare, or gathering the fallen grapes of his vineyard, depriving the poor

inquired about the truth of what she claimed. Surely the man against whom she sought justice was embarrassed and angry, and mounted his own gossip defense to her claims. Surely his friends spread false rumors about her—her immorality, incredibility, and ignorance. Slander was added to the merciless injustice she had suffered. But she kept coming back and coming back, as lonely and vulnerable as she had to have felt. Perhaps she developed a small following of elders who believed privately that she had been treated unjustly and mercilessly, but who still did not have the moral courage to stand and speak for her.

Eventually, the judge gave in and heard her case. Why? She was not going away. She was disrupting the proceedings. She was calling into question the legitimacy of the entire court. He gave her the "justice" she wanted to shut her up and make her go away.

Who knows what happened to her after she received her vindication.

The parallels between this parable, 2nd Chronicles 19 and Sirach 35, are striking. In 2 Chr 19:7, the king instructs the appointed judges to "let the fear of the LORD be upon you; take care what you do, for there is no perversion of justice with the LORD our God, or partiality . . . " Yet the judge in Jesus' parable had no fear of God and no respect for this widow. He was partial to the oppressor and was perverting justice. The writing from Sirach, an intertestamental writing known in Jesus' time and place, contrasts God as judge with humans as judges, just as Jesus' parable does. In Sir 35:16b–17, the Lord "will listen to the prayer of one who is wronged. He will not ignore the supplication of the orphan, or the widow when she pours out her complaint," in contrast to the judge in the parable who ignores the widow's supplications for so long. In Sir 35:21–22, "the prayer of the humble pierces the clouds, and it will not rest until it reaches its goal; it will not desist until the Most High responds and does justice for the righteous, and executes judgment. Indeed, the Lord will not delay, and like a warrior will not be patient until he crushes the loins of the unmerciful." Just as the "prayer" of the humble poor in Sir 35:21 would not "desist," so the widow in the parable "kept coming" until justice was granted. Just as the Lord in the passage from Sirach would "not delay" or be patient in repaying with vengeance, so God in Jesus' parable would not delay in granting justice (Luke 18:8).

There is at least one other striking parallel between the parable of Jesus and this passage from Sirach 35. In the parable at verses 7 and 8, the Greek word *ekdikésis* is used, which I believe is the only time this word appears in any parable. The NRSV translates the phrases that include this

enabled it. It would have left the wrongdoer in his self-justification and denial. Of course, justice to the widow was a great mercy to her. But the only chance the oppressor had in being transformed into a person who would turn from the conduct taught by the dominant narrative to become merciful would be to hold him accountable through the widow's suit. The appetite for power being what it was and is in some human beings, and the power of the dominant narrative being as pervasive as it was and is, it seems unlikely that the victory of the widow would begin to transform her oppressor. Through the Justice Ministry, we have represented very many such widows seeking justice and mercy against their abusers from the court system. We have had an easier time obtaining vindication than the widow in this parable. The immediate reaction of the abusers has almost always been to rail at the system and accuse the victim of lying and worse, even though we have tried to treat the abuser with respect and encouragement to repentance. Being held accountable did not seem to start a process of transformation for the abusers in most of our cases.

But there are always two parts of merciful justice and just mercy. One part is the offer; the other is the acceptance. Whether the oppressor in this parable or the abusers in our family violence suits will likely accept the just mercy of accountability being offered them, under the counternarrative of Jesus they are still always due the offer. Whether an individual accepts is something of an *agón* between him and the dominant narrative, and God.

**

The Parable of the Pharisee and the Tax Collector

9 He also told this parable to some who trusted in themselves that they were just and regarded others as of no account: 10 "Two men went up to the temple to pray, one a Pharisee and the other a tax collector. 11 The Pharisee, standing by himself, was praying thus, 'God, I thank you that I am not like other people: thieves, rogues, adulterers, or even like this tax collector. 12 I fast twice a week; I give a tenth of all my income.' 13 But the tax collector, standing far off, would not even look up to heaven, but was beating his breast and saying, 'God, be merciful to me, a sinner!' 14 I tell you, this man went down to his home justified rather than the other; for all who exalt themselves will be humbled, but all who humble themselves will be exalted." (Luke 18:9–14)

counter-narrative of Jesus. The word "rogue" of the NRSV is a translation of the Greek *adikos*. The Greek literally means "unjust." The Pharisee
thanks God that he is just while the *adikos* is not. But within the counter-
narrative, he fails to render the mercy to the *adikos* and the others that
they are due as a matter of God's justice. So indeed the Pharisee is unjust.

The Pharisee was quite merciful to the poor—the orphan, the widow, and the alien. The justice taught by Torah was that the orphan, the
alien, and the widow were due the Pharisee's tithes, and he obeyed. So he
was simultaneously just and merciful to them. But he did not accept that
his mercy was also due to "thieves, rogues, adulterers," and the "tax collector" in the parable. The sin of all those people was a failure to render
unto vulnerable people the mercy they were due as children of God. But
in judging who was due his mercy and who was not, the Pharisee was also
guilty of a lack of justice and mercy to thieves, rogues, adulterers, and
tax collectors. By his sense of superiority, his self-righteousness, and his
condemnations, he turned these children of God into "them." His judgment was that his own mercilessness toward "them" was not sinful, while
their mercilessness toward others was sinful. But all were guilty of the
same sins of injustice and mercilessness. As stated in verse 9 of the parable: the Pharisee trusted "in himself" to decide who was due mercy and
who was not. He was guilty of the same sin of lack of mercy as the others.
But unlike the tax collector in the parable, the Pharisee did not see his
sin, confess it, and repent of it. So he did not go down from the Temple
Mount acquitted of the sin. The sin continued.

What was the mercy due from the Pharisee to thieves, rogues,
adulterers, and the tax collector in the parable? To accept them as fellow
children of God, and to try to help them become merciful. Not just to
condemn and exclude, which would accomplish nothing for them. Not
just by keeping himself pure and separate, "standing by himself" (verse
1). Mercy toward the thieves, rogues, adulterers, and tax collector would
come from being in relation with them—befriending, mentoring, and
helping them find the way to being merciful through being merciful to
them. In this relationship, all could help all to be more merciful. This was
what Jesus did and taught. Mercy toward "them" would be to sit at table
with them, as Jesus was criticized by Pharisees for eating with tax collectors and sinners. (Luke 5:30.) The Pharisee seems to have been more
concerned with his own complete holiness than with his complete mercifulness. He thus created a false duality of holiness versus mercifulness.

due mercy rather than deciding the specific form of mercy that everyone was due under the counter-narrative of God. In his pride and self-satisfaction, he was not rendering unto himself what he was due—to become a thoroughly merciful person. The tax collector recognized his previous mercilessness and repented of it. The tax collector went from the temple resolving to treat the people vulnerable to him with the mercy they were due. In doing so, he rendered unto himself the greatest mercy—allowing himself to become a merciful and therefore just person.

Very many more Pharisees than tax collectors are in the modern American church and secular society. We follow the dominant narrative, deciding who is due our mercy and who is not, and who is and is not due being in our presence and in a relationship with us. Like the Pharisee, we believe ourselves to be due more of God's regard and protection than the people we see as rogues. We believe ourselves to be superior to others because of our accidents of birth—our families, our networks, our inherited positions, and our capabilities. And we believe ourselves to be superior to others because of their conduct, never asking what in their lives brought them to the conduct we condemn and fear. We give thanks to God that we are better than those who live the plight of the homeless, the addict, the convicted felon, the registered sex offender, the undocumented alien, the minimum wage earner, the recipient of food stamps, the unemployed, and the unmarried mother with children from multiple fathers. So we keep ourselves separated. We never learn what the lives of "them" are actually like. And we withhold the great blessings of our stunning virtue and shining personalities from them. In thinking and behaving in this way, like the Pharisee in the parable we deny the mercy that is due to them and to us. We remain complacently in our own mercilessness. The dominant narrative wins in our lives again.

**

The Parables of the Lost and Strayed Sheep

12 "What do you think? If a shepherd has a hundred sheep, and one of them has gone astray, does he not leave the ninety-nine on the mountains and go in search of the one that went astray? 13 And if he finds it, truly I tell you, he rejoices over it more than over the ninety-nine that never went astray. 14 So it is not the

criticism of him by the Pharisees and religious insiders is that he associated with people who were still sinners—who had not yet repented and reformed their lives. Jesus' saying in Luke 5:31–32 was a response to Pharisees who were complaining that he was eating with unrepentant sinners. Jesus was associating with those sinners by sharing a meal with them in order to move them to repent. He did not require them to repent before he would eat with them.

Through the Lord's Prayer, Jesus teaches his followers to pray: "And forgive us our debts as we also have forgiven our debtors . . . For if you forgive others their trespasses, your heavenly father will also forgive you. But if you do not forgive others, neither will your Father forgive your trespasses" (Matt 5:12, 14–15). Jesus said nothing there about repentance by the wrongdoer to the wronged before the wrongdoer is due forgiveness.

In Jesus' teachings repentance would not just mean thinking differently. Repentance would require that one's entire purpose and life would change. But I find no strict *quid pro quo* requirement in Jesus' teachings that restitution be made, that the victim be compensated, that what was lost be restored, or that an eye be given back for every eye taken before the wrongdoer is due to be restored to relationship and given a new start. Jesus' emphasis was upon letting the wrongdoer up, letting her start over with a fresh chance, letting her get beyond the past, and letting her be "born anew." For him, there was no requirement of repentance first, no requirement that the wrongdoer first recognize and acknowledge that what she had done was wrong and hurtful, no requirement that she first apologize and ask for forgiveness, and no requirement that she first promise not to repeat the hurt. Jesus' focus is upon the future, not on the past. And the focus of Jesus' life and teaching was for his followers on his way to be merciful to a wrongdoer by freely giving her the mercy of forgiveness and restoration.

But according to the dominant narrative of Jesus' and of our time, setting aside a hurtful wrong without punishment and restitution is not only unjust but also scandalous. Only after the victim has received in full what is due from the wrongdoer, only after the wrongdoer has paid an equitable price, and only after justice is therefore done should there be a chance for forgiveness and restoration to relationship. And this forgiveness and restoration, like all mercy, was and is optional. In no area is Jesus' narrative more counter to the dominant narrative than in the justice and mercy of repentance and forgiveness.

sinner with no assurance that the sinner would respond with repentance. The shepherd went anyway, taking all of the initiative and with the evident intention of inspiring the strayed sheep to repentance by the shepherd's merciful and risky love. This is much as Jesus was eager to eat with sinners before there was any sign of their repentance.

This is not the justice of the dominant narrative, then or now. Within our dominant narrative, the ninety-nine faithful, obedient sheep were due more protection and more attention, not less, from the shepherd. In fact, they were due all of the shepherd's protection and attention. The one strayed sheep was due nothing, because he had strayed. Within the dominant narrative, it's up to the strayed sheep to un-stray himself, to find his way back, to repent first, and to pull himself up by his own hoof-straps, before any welcome and restoration is due to this sheep from the shepherd and the other sheep. In the meritocracy of the dominant narrative, the faithful, obedient sheep were due the rewards of their faithful obedience. In the dominant narrative, the shepherd's abandonment of the faithful ninety-nine in a place of risk was an outrageous injustice. Under the dominant narrative, the faithful ninety-nine are the "little ones" who are due having their guardian angels continually in God's presence, not the faithless sinner in need of repentance.

But there is an additional view of this, which is even more provocative to our time and situation. It is suggested by Jesus' use of the "one" compared to the "ninety-nine."

The Pharisees and their followers, not Jesus' sinners, were in the numeric minority in that time. Josephus, the Jewish historian and collaborator with the Romans in the first century, estimated that there were perhaps 6,000 Pharisees in all of the Holy Land during this period, among between 1.5 and 2 million Jews there. Regardless of the exact numbers, the Pharisees were a tiny minority. The word "Pharisee" is believed to have been derived from ancient Greek and Aramaic for "separated." The Pharisees insisted that Torah required all Jews to "separate" themselves from all gentiles and even from non-righteous Jews by strictly observing Torah Sabbath, purity and tithing regulations. Pharisees believed in an oral Torah through which strict religious observances were expanded into every area of life. The vast majority of Jews who did not, and could not because of their poverty, observe all of these regulations were "sinners" with whom Pharisees avoided contact. Because of their disobedience to these regulations, the Pharisees considered that these "sinners" had strayed through sin. These sinners had lost themselves. The Pharisees

Jesus' strident condemnations of the Pharisees, the scribes, and their lawyers from Matthew 23 and Luke 11 seem anything but merciful. Perhaps these bitter condemnations more reflect the controversies between the communities of the early followers of the way and the synagogue in the remainder of the first century after Jesus was crucified. But accountability in the form of hard-spoken, truthful judgment can be merciful. And the repeated actions of Jesus in teaching and interacting with the Pharisees were undeniably merciful. This mercy, given the great damage that the Pharisees were doing to so many people because of their condemnations and exclusions, was certainly not due them under the dominant narrative of that time.

Another approach to this parable of the sheep can be rooted in the Book of Ezekiel. Regardless of whether the one lost or strayed sheep represented the Pharisees or the larger number of persons regarded by Pharisees as "sinners," passages from Ezekiel 34 have important language in common with Jesus' parable of the lost and strayed sheep. This may have provided Jesus with a resonate foundation for his parable.

> 1 The word of the Lord came to me: 2 Mortal, prophesy against the shepherds of Israel: prophesy, and say to them—to the shepherds: Thus says the Lord God: Ah, you shepherds of Israel who have been feeding yourselves! Should not shepherds feed the sheep? 3 You eat the fat, you clothe yourselves with the wool, you slaughter the fatlings; but you do not feed the sheep. 4 You have not strengthened the weak, you have not healed the sick, you have not bound up the injured, you have not brought back the strayed, you have not sought the lost, but with force and harshness you have ruled them. 5 So they were scattered, because there was no shepherd; and scattered, they became food for all the wild animals. 6 My sheep were scattered, they wandered over all the mountains and on every high hill; my sheep were scattered over all the face of the earth, with no one to search or seek for them.

> 7 Therefore, you shepherds, hear the word of the LORD: 8 As I live, says the Lord God, because my sheep have become a prey, and my sheep have become food for all the wild animals, since there was no shepherd; and because my shepherds have not searched for my sheep, but the shepherds have fed themselves, and have not fed my sheep; 9 therefore, you shepherds, hear the word of the LORD: 10 Thus says the Lord God, I am against the shepherds; and I will demand my sheep at their hand, and put a stop to their feeding the sheep; no longer shall the shepherds feed themselves. I will rescue my sheep from their mouths, so that they may not be food for them. 11 For

from predators, strengthened, healed, and searched for and brought back when they strayed. The sheep were not even due to be kept together by the shepherds. And between sheep and sheep, each animal was due to compete to feed on good pasture and drink from clean water while spoiling the pasture and the water supply for other sheep. Within the dominant narrative, each animal was due to be able to push the other animals away from good food and water with flank and shoulder, to butt the weak animals, and to scatter them far and wide.

Within the counter-narrative of the prophet Ezekiel—within the counter-narrative of God—the life of the flock was to be a community of covenant, not an *agón*. Just obligations were placed upon the shepherds and were due from the shepherds to the sheep. Because each sheep was in a relationship of trust with the shepherds and with the other sheep, just obligations were placed upon each sheep which were due to the shepherds and to every other sheep. These mutual, just obligations grew out of the relationships within the community, not from any competition. These were mutual, just obligations *to be merciful*.

The shepherds were *not* due to eat the fat of the sheep, to clothe themselves with the wool, to slaughter the fatlings, and to rule with force and harshness over their sheep. The shepherds were *not* due to prey upon their sheep. From the shepherds, each sheep was due to be protected from predators and from other sheep, and to be fed, strengthened, healed, searched for, and brought back when they strayed. Each sheep was due from every other sheep not to have their pasture and water source fouled, and not to be pushed away from pasture and water by the flank and shoulder of stronger sheep.

This writing from Ezekiel about the dominant narrative and the counter-narrative of God is relevant to our time. Consider the shepherd CEO of a large corporation with many sheep employees. Under today's dominant narrative, the CEO is due to eat of the fat created by the employees, and due to rule over them harshly by keeping their wages as low as he can while still maintaining a competent work force, by laying off large numbers of workers to maximize profits, and possibly even by closing their particular workplace to reduce labor costs further.

Within the setting of Jesus' telling of this parable, which was a response to the Pharisees' questioning of why Jesus spent so much time with and attention to sinners, Jesus was being asked about justice issues similar to the ones raised by the parable. Why are the sinners due so much more of your attention, protection, and encouragement than those of us

The strayed sheep is due more than withholding forgiveness until after an act of repentance that satisfies the flock and that includes a promise to conform to the flock's view of righteousness. Under the above passages of Ezekiel and Jesus' parable, any sheep is due being protected from any other sheep that would push her out. Any sheep is due being searched for even if the sheep chooses to stray. Any sheep is due rescue just because she is a cherished member of the flock. Jesus teaches that there is a just obligation to search mercifully for all the lost, excluded, and separated.

Perhaps the sheep was lost and strayed because she was judged, excluded, and separated. Perhaps she was lost because she was "pushed with flank and shoulder, and butted . . . until scattered . . . far and wide" (Ezek 34:21). Perhaps she was lost because of the oppressive theology and ethic of the dominant narrative of her time by which she is declared to be impure and defiled. Perhaps she was pushed out because she did not have the resources to observe the purity provisions of Torah. Perhaps she strayed by not accepting the mercilessness of the dominant narrative. To Jesus, the Pharisees and their victims were lost. To the Pharisees, Jesus was lost and Jesus was causing his followers to be lost. In this sense, this parable dovetails with Jesus' parable of the wheat and weeds (Matt 13:24–30). Who are we to judge who is weed and who is wheat? So who are we to "push with flank and shoulder" until others are "lost" and "strayed"? All are to be sought after and reunited, regardless of who is judged as having strayed or having remained faithful. No one is due exclusion from the nurture and protection of the flock.

Jesus also addresses whether the faithful ninety-nine sheep actually want the "lost" and "strayed" brought back to their flock. Probably the ninety-nine did not want their shepherd to act like God depicted in the passage in Ezekiel 34. It was a matter of "us" versus "them," of "ours" versus "theirs." Consider that a strayed sheep has likely been changed by the experience of being lost. The world will look and feel differently to that sheep after the experience of exclusion and separation, and perhaps after experiencing the thrill and cost of the freedom of cutting loose. That lost world may always beckon. The excluded-and-then-rescued sheep will be seen by himself and other sheep as different from the members of the flock. The returned sheep may even not agree that he was lost. He may not agree that he sinned by leaving to take another path while the sheep of the flock played it safe in their version of righteousness. Perhaps the lost sheep strayed because he had issues with the self-righteousness of the flock. Upon his return he may not agree that the sheep that remained in

the ninety-nine righteous sheep behind to go in search of a lost, strayed sheep merely because the one was lost, strayed, alone, and in need.

Any tight community, including a church, will experience the issues raised by these terse and brilliant parables.

When I was still in seminary, at my request my bishop appointed me to be the pastor to a small, dying, inner-city, Anglo church in an economically poor, increasingly Hispanic neighborhood. At first we had about twenty persons in our Sunday worship service, on a good Sunday. We didn't have a child to light the altar candles. The Sunday-school building, which had 15 rooms, was unused except for one meeting room and the kitchen. The congregation was dwindling because the members were dying, and because the Anglo members were afraid to invite their Hispanic neighbors to join. And they did not want to make any changes to their worship, their space, and their church life to attract new members from their neighborhood. The church was about to be the fourth United Methodist Church on the north side of the city to close. The faithful members of the church had every good memory of the past, and almost nothing good to say about the present. Most had worked in nearby packing plants or for an aircraft manufacturer. In the good old days, their neighborhood was almost completely Anglo and working class. Then their children grew up and moved away from the neighborhood as quickly as they could. The members became older and older and lost their vitality and health. They were spending more and more time in the hospital and dreaded moving into a nursing home. Inflation outstripped their fixed incomes. Their houses were aging along with them. Then poor Hispanics moved into the neighborhood and eventually took it over. The majority of the new neighbors were undocumented and spoke little English. Most of these newcomers were hard-working and family oriented, and took the best care that they could of their residences. But there were also some really violent gangs, drugs, burglaries, and even robberies, teen pregnancies, latchkey children, poverty, and, perhaps the most bothersome to the members, loud Tejano music blaring from homes and cars late into the night. When our old Anglo members came into the church, they wanted to step back into the safe and familiar past.

The children of these poor, Hispanic families were so much in need of hope, direction, and encouragement. If the church could serve the children, we could attract the parents as well. The children were being reared in a culture that was foreign to their parents, so their parents were ill-equipped to help their children find their way through all the

good. Ministry by the church "with" the homeless was a problem for some. When some members and clergy organized a worship service and breakfast that was attended by 80 to 120 downtown homeless early on Sunday mornings in the main building of the church, there was some fear of "them" that had to be addressed.

This was the single hour in the weekly life of the church that looked, to me at least, like my vision of the kingdom of God. It was the church's lone integrated hour—racially, ethnically, and economically. It was the sole hour in which everyone felt welcome. But the presence in the main church building of our unsheltered neighbors, who were often dirty and smelly, and who needed the use of the church bathrooms to clean and relieve themselves, made a number of our members and staff uncomfortable and even afraid. And when it was discovered that a very few registered sex offenders ("RSOs") were attending, the Sunday morning worship and breakfast for all of the homeless in the main church building was at risk of termination. Some parents and staff objected to having "RSOs" in the same building with our children, youth, and adults. To refer to the parable, it was good with most of the ninety-nine sheep for a few shepherds to go out from the flock's home pasture to seek and save the lost. But it was not good to bring these particular lost back to the home pasture of the ninety-nine. In fairness, there were many in the congregation who rejoiced when we brought them "home," but there were many who did not.

I am not the least bit critical in any way of anybody who wants to protect vulnerable children. It is a fact that I have spent most of my legal and ministerial career trying to protect abused children. I have personally dealt hundreds of times over the years with the results of violent abuse of children, including sexual abuse. But fear will always defeat mercy. The dominant narrative defeats mercy by inspiring and justifying fear. Jesus spent most of his ministry with "sinners." Sin comes in all shapes and sizes. Some of it is familiar and shared by those on the "inside." Some of it is foreign, unsettling, and even dangerous. Many insiders fear that all sin by the poor is dangerous. Regardless, fear can direct us completely away from Jesus' Way of mercy if we allow it to do so.

The Sunday morning worship and breakfast for our homeless in our main church building was preserved. Additional precautions were put in place by dedicated and faithful people. Hopefully some fears were assuaged. Fears are real, even if some might consider them unfounded and un-Christian. It's generally not helpful to grade someone else's fear. And

wages, the lack of the necessary job skills to make enough income to obtain their own roof, the lack of available subsidized housing, the continuing lack of family support, untreated mental illness, physical disability, addiction, flight from family violence, a felony record, being a registered sex offender, and because they compile a long misdemeanor record for criminal trespass while they are homeless. And they stay homeless just because they are homeless.

If a homeless person remains homeless for six months, the chances fall significantly that he or she will ever get out of the trap. The person fails to find a roof, falls into despair, and quits trying. Homelessness is like quicksand. If you fall in and struggle, it feels as if you are sinking deeper and deeper. So you just give up. Homelessness itself keeps the homeless from finding work that pays enough to get them out of homelessness. If you are homeless, you probably lack an address to put on a job application. You probably lack the clothing and hygiene to obtain a decent-paying job. You lack a place to leave all the possessions you have to carry on your back while you go on an interview or while you work. If a prospective employer discovers you are homeless, the employer will lose interest unless he is looking to hire the homeless to take advantage of them. You likely have a lack of personal transportation, so showing up on time for any appointment or starting time is more than a challenge. You likely can't access treatment for your mental illness, or accommodation for your physical disability. Or you are a teenager who was kicked out of your mother's house by your mother's new boyfriend. Or you are a woman fleeing from family violence, and you have no job history and no employment skills because your abuser kept you utterly dependent upon him. Or you are a long-term employee who was seriously injured away on the job, lost your job when you didn't recover quickly enough, and cannot find new work because of your age and your lingering impairment.

Our homeless friends tell me that the worst aspect of their lives is not exposure to the cold, heat, wet and wind. It's not their markedly decreased life expectancy. It's not your own smell and dirt. It's not the dangers of being on the street. It's not the trouble finding a place to wash and defecate. The worst is that other people who aren't homeless won't even look you in the face. People are suspicious of you just because you are homeless, as if homelessness is your only defining characteristic. I'd say that the homeless are treated like stray dogs except that many more people will act mercifully to a stray dog than to a homeless person.

there are a few RSOs among the homeless, all homeless are feared and shunned.

I have helped put men in prison for rape for decades. In the Methodist Justice Ministry, we frequently try to protect and help adult and child victims of sexual assault. I suspect that I am as familiar as any non-victim can be with the toll of this conduct. But the complete shunning of registered sex offenders by churches, regardless of what precautions might be taken, is, I am convinced, utterly against the counter-narrative of Jesus.

In this parable Jesus teaches that we are called to seek and bring back the strayed even before they repent. This issue of welcoming the lost into our church home would be less challenging if we could first require them to present fruits of their repentance. But we are taught to seek, find, and bring back the strayed to our home in order to *then* move them to repentance and new life. The sequence is critical.

This is important as well to my clients' response when the abusers of their children and themselves say they are sorry and ask for forgiveness. What of mercy to the abuser by the abused? What of the call of the abused to be merciful? Must the abused woman gather her abused children in her arms and run down the road as the prodigal abuser approaches? Must the abused sheep be merciful by welcoming the abusive sheep back "home" whenever the abuser is found and brought back by the shepherd? Is that what the mercy of Jesus requires?

I hope not. Mercy is due to the victims of the abuser, and mercy is due to the abuser. That mercy takes different forms at different times. Part of the mercy to the abuser is an accountability that is intended to persuade the abuser of his wrongdoing, and to face him with the hurt and harm he has caused. By his abuse, the abuser has been merciless to the woman and the children, but also to his true self. He has allowed himself to become a terror and a monster to those he should have been nurturing and protecting. In order for him to repent and be born anew, he must see and appreciate his own abusiveness. To bring the abuser to this repentance and reform would be the greatest of mercies to him, for it would also make him merciful instead of merciless. And the mercy of protection to the abused woman and children will be much different than the mercy of restorative accountability to the abuser.

Surely the lost and strayed of the parable of the sheep include the mentally ill, the felon, the registered sex offender, the homeless and the abuser. The dominant narrative says have no mercy for these lost. They

you.' 30 But he refused; then he went and threw him into prison until he should pay the debt. 31 When his fellow slaves saw what had happened, they were greatly distressed, and they went and reported to their lord all that had taken place. 32 Then his lord summoned him and said to him, 'You wicked slave! I forgave you all that debt because you pleaded with me. 33 Should you not have had mercy on your fellow slave, as I had mercy on you?' 34 And in anger his lord handed him over to be tortured until he should pay his entire debt. (Matt 18:21–34)

Within the dominant narrative, there is no relationship between justice and mercy. In Jesus' counter-narrative, illustrated again in this parable, mercy and justice are interrelated and interdependent. Receipt of mercy creates a just duty to be merciful.

A "talent" was a weight of gold, silver, or copper. Ten thousand talents would be more than two hundred metric tons of gold or silver. One talent was equivalent to about six thousand *denarii* in weight, equivalent to about six hundred day's pay. So the first slave's debt was about sixty million *denarii* and sixty thousand days of work—truly impossible to repay.

Many may question why the king would ever have loaned him so much or allowed him to accrue that much debt. Regardless, the debt was so huge that it could not be repaid in one hundred sixty years, more than twice an entire lifetime. Within the dominant narrative, the king was due to be paid. The slave was due to be punished because he could not pay what was due to the king. He was most certainly not due the startling mercy of having his debt wiped clean.

Under the dominant narrative of Jesus' time and certainly of our time, the conduct of the forgiven slave in refusing to forgive the much lesser debt of the second was shrewd and just. It was just good business. The forgiven slave was due whatever profit he could make as a competitive business person. That he had received such a windfall of forgiveness did not change his relationship or duties with his own debtors. In Jesus' time, perhaps the hearers of this parable would have associated the slaves with tax farmers. Tax farmers were often slaves. Under this understanding, the trusted slave who owed the huge debt could have won a contract to collect taxes for an entire Roman province, explaining the huge amount. This would have required him to agree to pay the ten thousand talents to the king who entrusted him. The slave's ability to pay back his debt and to make a profit would have come from collecting more in taxes than he

Or suppose that a government in the developing world had incurred a huge debt to the World Bank in order to provide basic governmental services to its citizens through purchase of needed electrical, water purification, and medical equipment from suppliers in the developing world. Suppose the developing-world government expected to be able to raise the funds to pay back the debt by taxing its people. And suppose that the government was not able to raise that money because its people remained impoverished, and because the leaders of the government siphoned off a chunk of the government's income through corruption. Then suppose that the World Bank forgave the debt completely, with mixed motives of mercy and the economic viability of the businesses selling to the government. Within the dominant narrative of the corrupt governmental leaders, there would have been nothing unexpected or even wrong about their continuing to demand the citizens pay their taxes and to seize their assets if they failed. Within that narrative, there would be nothing unjust for these leaders to enrich themselves through the corruption that is standard operating procedure within that dominant narrative. But under Jesus' counter-narrative, the mercy given by the World Bank creates a just duty of the third-world government and leaders to forgive the tax debt of its people and of its third-world suppliers.

Or suppose that a married man is a serial adulterer, and that he is constantly on the prowl for one-night conquests of other women. Suppose that his repeated infidelities are exposed, that his wife sues him for divorce, and that she is about to be awarded a very disproportionate share of the considerable community property because of the husband's misconduct. Then suppose that the husband begs for forgiveness and reconciliation. The wife relents and gives the man another chance, partly because she still loves him, but mostly for the sake of their four children. The divorce suit is dismissed. A year later, the husband learns that his wife had a brief sexual relationship with another man when the husband was engaged in his serial conquests. The wife asks for forgiveness but the husband refuses. The husband uses this to return to his predatory ways. He tells her that if she sues for divorce again and tries to obtain more than half of the community property, he will expose her infidelity and embarrass her paramour. The forgiveness she extended him for many, many more infidelities has no effect upon him. Within the dominant narrative as he has received it, he is merely pursuing what he is due by looking out for himself. Within the dominant narrative he lives by, the more sexual conquests, the more successful and happy the man. But within

own self not to be merciful to us, and that God would never be unjust in this way no matter how merciless we are toward others. We live as if the mercies we receive are not the free, astonishing, undue mercies of the sovereign of all creation. And we live as if the only just obligation created upon us by God's undue mercies is for us to personally receive and enjoy them, with nothing due from us in return to God, to God's creation, or to God's other children. We live as if our passing on the mercy we have received from God is merely optional. In short, we live by the dominant narrative.

The free, undue mercy of God creates a just obligation on us to mimic God's mercy without calculation of who and who is not due this mercy. We cannot pay our debt to God directly for the undue mercies we receive from God. So we are due to pay off that debt with the same mercy God has freely lavished upon us, by lavishing our mercies upon our brothers and sisters regardless of whether we judge that our brothers and sisters are due our mercy. The only question will be the form that these mercies will take.

This truth about God's justice and mercy, and the creation of an obligation that is due by the gift of what is not due, is as paradoxical as most of the truths of God revealed in Scripture. You can only gain your life by losing it. You become the greatest by becoming the least. The greatest power is in powerlessness. Receipt of free and unjust mercy creates a just obligation to be merciful.

According to the dominant narrative, the first slave was completely within his prerogative by demanding payment from the second slave, payment that the first slave was indeed due. But that right was upended by the king's mercy to the first slave, which is part of a radical counter-narrative. The king's mercy—this counter-narrative—reversed the right of the first slave to receive payment for what he was due to an obligation of the first slave to be merciful by forgiving the debt. The king's mercy changed everything. "You received without payment; give without payment" (Matt 10:8).

It is like our lives. We were not due being created. We were certainly not due being created into this magnificent planet Earth. When God granted us life, we received a completely undue mercy and an utterly free gift. But having received this undue mercy, mercy is due from us to others.

Is verse 34 an unflattering portrait of God? "He handed him over to be tortured until he paid his entire debt." Given that the amount of the

evildoers to the hilt. We do not turn the other cheek. We do not love our enemies; we obliterate them and theirs. We are supremely anxious about our possessions and about tomorrow. We give to the poor only begrudgingly if at all. We spend almost all of our money and resources on ourselves. We don't eat with sinners, which is to say people who do not accept and triumph in the dominant narrative. We try to put as much distance as we can between ourselves and outsiders. We never search for the lost sheep. We live as if our value and happiness lie only in accumulating the most stuff, the most enduringly youthful appearance and the most transient pleasures. We live as if we are due whatever we can get and others are not due whatever they cannot. So we desire that God will never hold us accountable. And we fear that God will.

The second reason that we comfortable American churchians believe that God is only merciful and not just is that we see no clear signs that God holds us or others accountable when we are merciless. The prophet Zephaniah wrote:

> I will search Jerusalem with lamps, and I will punish the people who rest complacently on their dregs, those who say in their hearts, "The LORD will not do good, nor will he do harm." (Zeph 1:12)

Zephaniah was writing about those who believed that God is neither merciful nor just because God is just not involved at all in creation. I think it is easy for middle and upper class American churchians to believe that God is merciful because our lives are generally so blessed. And because our lives are generally so easy, it is also easy to believe that God is mercifully behind our ease and comfort. It is no challenge to believe that God is merciful when we are able to satisfy every material and transient desire flung upon us by the media of the dominant narrative. It is much more of a challenge for my impoverished clients to believe that God is merciful.

As for God's justice, we read in every newspaper stories about evil, terror, hate crimes, refugees fleeing oppression, violence against innocent "collaterals," child abuse, sexual exploitation, drug selling and addiction, cheating, fraudulent business practices, narcissistic accumulation of wealth, and endless self-promotion. The thriving of those who are merciless has always been hard to square with a just God. So we see in many of Jesus' teachings, including this parable, a persistent hope and plea that

by whether we were just and occasionally merciful under the dominant narrative of our time, not under the counter-narrative of Jesus.

Is God so merciful that God will never render unto us the accountability we are due for our merciless indifference? Is there an unalterable conflict between God's justice and God's mercy, just as there is between the justice and mercy of the dominant narrative?

Does human conduct count for so little in God's eyes that God will never hold us accountable for our mercilessness? What if such accountability would serve to make us and others more merciful? We live as if we will never have to pay a debt to God for being indifferently unmerciful, as if there will never be any accountability for our mercilessness. Is God's nature this one dimensional? Is God such a bad father? Or does God's merciful nature include a will that we be made merciful? Does God's nature also include the mercy and justice to hold us accountable when we fail to render to others the mercy we have been rendered, in order to make us and others merciful? This parable, as so many in Matthew's Gospel, says there will be accountability. If we heed this teaching, and it inspires and leads us to be more merciful, we have not only received but have accepted a great mercy.

Are God's ethical standards identical to ours? Or are we called to mirror God's mercy but not God's judgment? Perhaps.

Is there a tension between mercy and accountability? Is there any tension between mercy and accountability carried out in a way to be merciful to the victim and to the wrongdoer? What shape should that merciful accountability take, circumstance to circumstance?

**

The Parable of the Merciful and Just Landowner

¹ "For the kingdom of heaven is like a landowner who went out early in the morning to hire laborers for his vineyard. ² After agreeing with the laborers for the usual daily wage, he sent them into his vineyard. ³ When he went out about nine o'clock, he saw others standing idle in the marketplace; ⁴ and he said to them, 'You also go into the vineyard, and I will pay you whatever is right.' So they went. ⁵ When he went out again about noon and about three o'clock, he did the same. ⁶ And about five o'clock he went out and found others standing around; and he said to them, 'Why are you standing here idle all day?' ⁷ They said to

the critical term of the contract with the later hired workers at verse 4 ("I will pay you whatever is just") is vague and unenforceable because it gives the vineyard owner all the discretion to decide the amount of pay. But the setting is not modern America, and this contract term illustrates the unequal bargaining power of the owner and the workers. More to the point, this vagueness is part of the genius of the parable, setting the stage for an apparent tension between competing versions of justice and mercy.

Until the shocking end of the parable in which the landowner violates the dominant narrative of Jesus' time by the amounts he pays the workers, the relationship between the landowner and the laborers, as well as among the laborers, is competitors within an *agón*. The workers were selling their labor for as high a wage as they can each extract, and the landowner is offering as low a wage as he can for their work. The laborers see this as a zero sum contest; the more some other group of laborers is paid, the less my group will be paid. There is only so much in wages that can be paid. There was no hint that this was a transaction between members of a covenantal community. And there was no hint of any covenantal relationship among the laborers. They were competitors against one another, each competing to be hired as soon as he could to be "due" more pay for more work. So until the surprising and upsetting end of the parable, when the landowner openly declares what he will pay to each worker, this parable was all about justice—what each worker was "due"—under the dominant narrative of that time.

At the end of the workday, the landowner directs his manager to line up the workers so each could be paid in the presence of the other laborers. This in itself may have been shocking to the hearers. I have worked in private law firms in which it was a violation of firm rules for one employee to disclose to other employees what a specific employee was being paid. This rule was to reduce complaints, to limit demands to give raises to equalize pay among equals, and to reinforce the power and prerogatives of the owners of the firm.

Even more surprising, the owner has the workers who worked the least number of hours be paid first, so the ones who had "borne the burden of the day and the scorching heat" longer witnessed how much the other workers were paid. If the owner had reversed the order, presumably the workers who had worked the longest and received the *denarius* that they had agreed to as their daily wage would have been gone and not seen the shocking mercy of the owner to the other workers. The owner was intentionally causing controversy to teach a lesson about mercy.

would learn to be merciful. As well as receiving mercy, they were each due to be made merciful.

This parable is another one that teaches that God's justice and mercy are fused. What we are all due is mercy and to be made merciful. What could be more different from the dominant narrative of our time than the way the vineyard owner paid and interacted with the laborers?

**

The Parable of the Sheep and Goats

31 "When the Son of Man comes in his glory, and all the angels with him, then he will sit on the throne of his glory. 32 All the nations will be gathered before him, and he will separate people one from another as a shepherd separates the sheep from the goats, 33 and he will put the sheep at his right hand and the goats at the left. 34 Then the king will say to those at his right hand, 'Come, you that are blessed by my Father, inherit the kingdom prepared for you from the foundation of the world; 35 for I was hungry and you gave me food, I was thirsty and you gave me something to drink, I was a stranger and you welcomed me, 36 I was naked and you gave me clothing, I was sick and you took care of me, I was in prison and you visited me.' 37 Then the righteous will answer him, 'Lord, when was it that we saw you hungry and gave you food, or thirsty and gave you something to drink? 38 And when was it that we saw you a stranger and welcomed you, or naked and gave you clothing? 39 And when was it that we saw you sick or in prison and visited you?' 40 And the king will answer them, 'Truly I tell you, just as you did it to one of the least of these who are members of my family, you did it to me.' 41 Then he will say to those at his left hand, 'You that are accursed, depart from me into the eternal fire prepared for the devil and his angels; 42 for I was hungry and you gave me no food, I was thirsty and you gave me nothing to drink, 43 I was a stranger and you did not welcome me, naked and you did not give me clothing, sick and in prison and you did not visit me.' 44 Then they also will answer, 'Lord, when was it that we saw you hungry or thirsty or a stranger or naked or sick or in prison, and did not take care of you?' 45 Then he will answer them, 'Truly I tell you, just as you did not do it to one of the least of these, you did not do it to me.' 46 And these will go away into

oppressed. There is no hint that they had cause the needy to be in need. They had just not been merciful. They had been indifferent. This is also like the rich man in the parable of the rich man and Lazarus.

Within the counter-narrative of this parable, the parable of the Good Samaritan and the parable of the rich man and Lazarus, we never have the right to judge who is due our mercy based upon their relationship to us or their conduct. To the extent that Matthew witnesses that Jesus taught that God withholds mercy at the judgment when it is not due to the merciless, it is only God who may and can do this. This is also like the parable of the wheat and tares (Matt 13:24–30). The requirement to be merciful to the needy mentions nothing of their ethnicity, religious choices, nationality, race, behavior, personal responsibility for their need, poor choices, virtue, laziness, or whether they would respond as we wish to our mercy. Mercy is due solely because of their need.

As I state above, whether to be merciful is never an issue in the counter-kingdom of Jesus. How to be merciful is always the only issue. How to balance the merciful needs of the needy we encounter is the issue. And these "hows" are not to be decided by the dominant narrative.

Within this parable, which is Jesus' last teaching in Matthew's Gospel and therefore his closing argument in his trial of earthly life, orthodox belief, faith in Jesus and his atoning death, confessing and asking for forgiveness, contributing to the church building fund, regularly attending worship and receiving the sacraments, and avoiding violation of all ten commandments play no part in getting you into the sheep flock at the final judgment. All that matters was whether you used whatever talents and capabilities you had received, and the fruits of those talents and abilities, to be merciful to those in need. Nothing else matters.

Consider how different not just the history of the church but also all of human history would have been if this "Parable of the Last Judgment" had been *the* primary criteria for the Christian way.

Heretics would never have been tortured and burned at the stake for wrong belief. To the extent that torture and burning could ever be justified within the counter-narrative, which it cannot, the criteria for torture would have been whether the candidates for punishment had failed to be merciful to the needy. But of course that would mean that the merciless were themselves in need of mercy and of being made merciful, not torture and death. So any torturers and the stake-burners would be exposed to the same punishment for their mercilessness in torturing and burning.

motivation in their mercy. They were merciful only because of their empathy at the need of the recipients, and the joy it brought them to alleviate suffering. The just in the parable were not merciful because the hungry, thirsty, alien, naked, and ill were judged by the just to have been innocent of their plight and therefore deserving of mercy. The just did not even know that Jesus was with and in the recipients. So despite the proclamation of terrible judgment for those who were merciless in their earthly lives, this fear had played no motive for the mercy of the merciful. They were merciful only because of the need of the recipients, their empathy with the needy, their love of mercy, and the joy they experienced in being merciful. In this sense, they were like God (Luke 6:36). God is not merciful because of a fear of punishment or hope for reward. Who can punish or reward God? God is merciful because of the need of the recipients, God's love of mercy, God's merciful nature, and God's joy in mercy.

Recall the colloquy between Jesus and the "lawyer" that led to Jesus' telling of the parable of the good Samaritan (Luke 10:25–29). The lawyer was trying to reduce the types and numbers of the "neighbor" whom he was required by Torah to love as himself. As I recount above, the debate between rabbinical schools in Jesus' time was that only Jews, or only righteous Jews who followed Torah rigorously, were "neighbors" deserving of our love. Jesus exploded any limitation on our duty of mercy. One of the great scandals of Jesus' ministry was that he was merciful through his teaching, presence, feeding, table fellowship, touch, and healing to everyone without limitation.

In the same way and under the same urge, Christians through the centuries have tried to limit the needy who are due mercy from Christians under this parable of Jesus. Some have said that this parable was the product of the early church and not of Jesus, and that the "least of these" whom Christians were called to love were only members of the persecuted, early Christian community. Some argue that these "least" to whom we are called now to be merciful are limited to members of our church.

There is no basis for these limitations. The parable does not state or support any limitation upon whom we Christians are due to be merciful. It says just the opposite. The motivation behind seeking to limit the people to whom our mercy is due is the same as the motivation behind the questioning of Jesus by the lawyer in Luke 10. It is the same motivation by which we, under the influence of the dominant narrative, limit those to whom we are called by Jesus to be merciful—to ourselves, our families, or maybe, sometimes, our close friends.

of Matthew 25, all these disciples of all nations were judged based upon whether they had followed Jesus' commandments of merciful conduct. But given that these disciples in all the nations would have encountered many in need in their nations who were not followers of Jesus, there is no basis for limiting those to whom Christians were and are commanded to be merciful. Part of what Jesus is saying in this parable is that every person of every nation is called and obligated to be merciful, because all peoples and nations have the needy and suffering in their midst.

This parable is indeed the fitting final argument of the trial of Jesus' life. It is the ultimate collapse of God's justice and God's mercy into one truth and way. It is an answer to those who see justice as a matter of reciprocity from within the dominant narrative. In this reciprocal view, acting justly requires treating the other as they have treated you and yours. If someone does something for you, then the justice of the dominant narrative requires you to do the same for them as well. If one is merciful to you, you are due to be merciful to them. The other side of this argument is that the other is not due mercy from you if they have never been merciful to you. Under this system of calculation, the only time I am motivated to be merciful to you is when I am looking to set up a reciprocal obligation of mercy from you to me. This is one form of justice within the dominant narrative.

The very last statement Jesus makes to his disciples before his resurrection, is, "and remember, I am with you always, to the end of the age" (Matt 28:20). But where and how is he always with us until the Judgment? He tells us in Matthew 25:40, 45: "Truly I tell you, just as you did it to the least of these my brothers, you did it to me . . . Truly I tell you, just as you did not do it to the least of these, you did not do it to me." Until the end of the age, Jesus is with us in the hungry, the thirsty, the stranger, the naked, the sick, and the imprisoned. All of these are not just Jesus' brothers and sisters. They are Jesus himself. As a matter of just reciprocity, to whom is mercy due from us more than to the eternal and divine Word who became flesh, who emptied himself of divinity to become our slave, who suffered our human frailties and fears, who made himself brother to the homeless, the sick, and the shunned, who taught and showed us mercy above all, who fed us and healed us, who showed us the nature of the Father and of the Way, who was tortured and killed for our sake by the tools of the dominant narrative, who defeated that narrative and death itself, and who is with us still? What is Jesus due from me and from you

CHAPTER 8

If There Is No Mercy, There Is No Justice

CAN WE READ IN these parables that Jesus tells us that he would die for our sins so that we need not be merciful and just according to God's counter-narrative? Where in these parables does Jesus tell us that we would be responding faithfully to his central message at Mark 1:15—"The time is fulfilled and the kingdom of God has come near; repent and believe in the good news"—merely by believing the right doctrine about his divinity and crucifixion, and by being "good" by the standards of justice and mercy of the *agón* of the dominant narrative? Or merely by being good churchians who tithe and attend worship regularly?

"Why do you call me 'Lord, Lord,' and not do what I tell you?" Jesus asks us at Luke 6:46.

Under the dominant narrative, justice and mercy have no connection. Indeed, they are in conflict. Mercy undercuts the so-called justice of the dominant narrative. The justice of the dominant narrative is without mercy, and the mercy taught by the dominant narrative is rare and weak. To follow the title of this book, in the world created by the dominant narrative, there is no mercy, and there is no true justice. Under this narrative, we are each due whatever we can get, and not due what we can and do not. Mercy is only occasional and optional; otherwise it would undermine the efficiency of the system of the dominant *agón* to produce more things and more transient pleasures. This dominant narrative would reduce all children of God to soulless and heartless competitors in a contest for these things and transient pleasures that do not satisfy. Produced by this narrative, the competition is unjust and merciless, preordaining millions of children and adults to be losers of the contest by their accidents of birth, and declaring that this random injustice is only just. This narrative appeals primarily to human predation, fear and suspicion. The

moments in this acquisition or consumption, worrying that we do not have enough of what will never truly satisfy us, when we already have far more than we need and far more than is good for our souls. We are conditioned by the dominant narrative to vote only our self-interest. Our self-interests are only to acquire all the things and pleasures we can, and to gain an advantage over our competitors. The dominant narrative teaches us that we should only rarely be merciful, and that we should be suspicious and condemning of people in need, even of children in need. The life necessarily growing out of this narrative is unsatisfying. As much as we gorge ourselves on it, the fruit of this tree is dry, tasteless, juiceless and unfulfilling. As soon as we acquire one thing or one pleasure, we only want more and more. The dominant narrative conditions us to be like spoiled children on Christmas morning, tearing open the wrappings on present after present, feeling dissatisfied when there are no more to unwrap, and never enjoying any of them. Fear, violence, acrimony, drug and alcohol addiction are on the rise. We lock our doors and hide from our neighbors. The works of the dominant narrative are "enmities, strife, jealousy, anger, quarrels, dissensions, factions, [and] envy" (Gal 5:19–21).

Within the counter-narrative of Jesus, we work to serve. We choose careers of service, or we use the money we make in highly paying jobs first to provide for the necessities for ourselves and our families and the rest in mercy to those who are in need. We choose to live more modestly, choosing smaller homes and less expensive cars, and eschewing shallow pleasure and impulse buying, in order to increase what we can give. Most of all, we give of ourselves, opening ourselves to *see, feel,* and *share* the lives of all of our brothers and sisters, and all of the children within the covenantal community. We worry about other people's children. We learn to open ourselves and to take pleasure in the wider moments of love and sacrifice, and in the new relationships and visions that grow out of these. We teach our children to see and feel the lives—the struggles, the nobilities, the hard work, the sacrifices, the hopelessness, and the perseverance—of those born into need. We stop judging the poor for acting as the comfortable do routinely. For those of us who must work at low paying jobs, and who have no excess beyond the basic needs of the family, we serve with our encouragement, our understanding, our presence and our sharing. Out of this grows a community, not an *agón*. The fruit of the counter-narrative of Jesus is "love, joy, peace, patience, kindness, generosity, faithfulness, gentleness and self-control" (Gal 5:22–23).

Christians are called in and through the counter-narrative of Jesus, first and last of all, to intercede everywhere for suffering children, women, and men, for a suffering creation, and for our suffering God.

In the first sentence of chapter 1 of this book, I wrote: "Anyone who doesn't recognize that life is unjust and merciless is a fool." I realize that such a statement begs the question of how an omnipotent, just, and merciful God could allow the random, merciless injustice of life to continue, particularly to children. I have no answer to this question beyond the life and teachings of the One whom we Christians believe was and is the Son of God. It is clear from this life and teachings that God does not will such random, merciless injustice to continue. And it is clear from Jesus' life and teachings that a response of God to this merciless injustice is the creation of a community of God's merciful justice and just mercy. And herein lies the greatest difference between the dominant narrative of America and God's counter-narrative.The dominant narrative embraces life as an unjust arena and a contest for things and pleasures that it inspires. It claims that the resulting consequence of the contest—merciless injustice—is beneficial and just. The counter-narrative of God and Jesus proclaims that the merciless injustices of human life and of the dominant narrative are evils that need to be transformed and from which we all need to be saved.

grabbing at him and us, almost pulling our garments off of us, scratching our skin and tearing our tunics. And some would fall in our path to plead with him to stop and touch them. Their strength seemed doubled by their desperation and hope. There were the blind and crippled, and pallid men carried on pallets. There were men and women with twisted limbs. There were men and women whose entire bodies were covered by their robes. Only their hands reached out from under the cloth to grasp at him and at us. These were probably lepers. Usually, people would draw back from any contact with a leper. But these people were so desperate that they were heedless of the uncleanness in their midst. And all around us, from every throat, rose the cry, "Master, have mercy on me, have mercy on me," or "have mercy upon my child, or my friend, or my wife, or my grandmother!"

When his ministry had first started, he might never have made it to the sea at all. He would have stayed right there for the entire day in the midst of the crush. He would have tried to heal and give a word of hope for every person there. It wasn't just the numbers of people. The number never went down. People who had been touched by him would not leave his presence. And more people came and came. It was the time that every person demanded and the time that he would spend with each person. He couldn't heal everyone who pleaded for his mercy. I never, ever saw him able to heal a person with a twisted limb from an old, bad broken bone. But when he touched people with fever, or blind or deaf people, or the unconscious, or the lepers, or the possessed, and they did not heal, he would not let himself give up. He would stay with them, trying, until they moved away from him or others in the crowd pulled them away from him.

Failing to heal a child was the hardest on him. You could see the energy draining out of him. You could see the pain and disappointment of any unhealed person pouring into him, but particularly of a child. We tried to protect him. We tried to be a buffer to keep the press off of him. He was a small man, wiry but light. He needed protecting. But he was heedless and unappreciative of our efforts. His focus was on the eyes of everyone there. I wondered how this much mercy could survive. He made no distinction between who might deserve his mercy and who might not. He made no distinction between whom he might be able to heal and whom he probably would not.

As his ministry went on, it seemed to us that his first goal became giving words of hope instead of healing. It tortured him when he could

a ring of us made a kind of human fence to keep others from swimming to the boat. The Master had clambered back into the boat and sat in the front, facing the crowd on the shore with his head down and his eyes closed until they quieted.

Then he began to teach them in parables, parables that all of us who had been with him from the beginning had heard many times before. And as he taught there was murmuring among the crowd because many did not understand, and because more wanted healing not words. After he had finished speaking, he sat silently and motionless for a very long time in the bow of the boat. Those of us who were with him in the boat saw that his eyes were closed and his lips were moving as if in a secret conversation. We knew then that he was in conversation with *Abba*. And we knew better than to interrupt him. Then he was asleep, folded up like a ball in the bow, his cloak covering him, overcome by exhaustion from the suffering he had absorbed from the crowd. Slowly, the people in the crowd on the bank sat down where they were to wait.

The day began to cool. The wind began to freshen. The sun was in its last quarter of the day. It was long past the midday meal. The Master slept a long time. He had been losing weight over the last months and had energy only in bursts before he would need to pray and sleep. I sometimes feared that his exposure to so much suffering and illness every single day was going to kill him. He gave so much of his own food away that he was not taking enough in to keep his weight up. Those of us with him in the boat had also eaten nothing all day. Some of us were quietly discussing whether to swim and wade to shore to get some bread and fish to eat. Two other boats were alongside our boat. One of us swam to the other boats to see what food they had on board. On the shore, dozens and dozens of people still sat, like sheep waiting for the shepherd to come back and lead them to pasture. It seemed that, as usual, we were going to have to put out into the water and sail for a distance to find a place where we could sleep undisturbed by the suffering.

One of the other boats contained enough bread to feed all of us a little. We shared that as the Master continued to sleep. The daylight faded and it became cold. The wind picked up, blowing onshore from the south. This was the time of day when we had once sailed into the sea to fish all night. The boats began to bob and rock.

As the wind picked up and the darkness deepened, a faint wailing reached us from the southeast. The night came on, and the cry grew a bit stronger. The Master stirred. He sat up and asked for water. He drank it

I felt ashamed. I crawled back to the helm. The sail up, we made way to the southeast. To the land of the Gerasenes.

The distance to sail was many miles. It would take more than the entire night to sail against the wind to the other side. That was if the wind did not die, or a sudden storm did not blow up, or the wind did not change course. Then . . . who knew. All three of the boats had shallow drafts, very tender to the waves and the wind. The boats were overloaded with us. Many of us had once made our living on that sea by fishing all night. That is how we had heard that possessed man's wails before. When the wind was from the east generally and we were fishing in the northern part of the sea, all night long we could hear his cries of torment coming from the east.

We were accustomed to the pitching of the boat, to the need to suddenly shift our own weights to keep from capsizing. But most of us were not fishermen. And when the wind picked up, we just had to ride it out. Some of our company became ill. All were afraid of drowning. Cries from inside our boat matched the wailing of the man from the Gerasenes. The Master called out, "Just trust. *Abba* did not bring us this far to die tonight."

The wind lessened but still blew. We had been blown out into the center of the sea. As the hours past and we were maneuvering against the wind by shifting our weight, those who were not fishermen began to complain again. A storm blew up . . . in the boat. The fishermen among us were answering the questions of the others about the man we were sailing to save. Arguments sprang up. "This is dangerous. Why does this possessed, unclean gentile deserve to be saved and we to die?" Some admonished those who complained. "Do you follow the Master or not? Do you follow him only when it is to your own advantage? He has taught us to have mercy on those in need. We are doing that." "But why to him and not to us?" they asked.

On the second watch, we finally arrived at the land of the Gerasenes. We were exhausted, wet and cold. There was vomit washing around the bottom of the boat. The Master was crouching in the bow as the boat came closer to shore, peering up into the cliff above the spit of sand. The boat slid onto sandy bottom and crunched to a rest. The other two boats slid along either side. All of us in the boats also peered up the cliff to catch first sight of the possessed man. I had only seen him at a great distance. I imagined a modern Goliath with eyes like a goat, and horns and snout like a hog, wanting to attack and devour us.

face. He lunged forward and wrapped his arms around the Master's body, crying. The Master sat backward awkwardly, his knees forward and his legs under him. The man crawled so his knees were bent and beside the Master's legs. The Master cradled him against his chest, rocking him. He began stroking the man's filthy hair. Many minutes passed. We could hear the Master singing to him softly.

We sat in the boats watching, transfixed, but still too afraid to get out. None of us had ever seen anything like this. Most never wanted to see anything like it ever again.

People who lived in the nearest village made their way down the cliff. Some swineherds were also there from the region. They had no idea who the Master was. They probably thought we were just more Hebrew fisherman who'd had boat problems. But when they saw who it was that the Master was cradling, they were afraid. They drew back as if they expected the man to kill the Master at any moment. They were talking frantically among themselves.

The Master stood. He called out to them, "There is no longer any reason to be afraid of this man. He is your brother. He is no longer possessed. He needs your welcome. He needs your mercy." The local people drew back, disbelieving. They were still afraid of the man and afraid of the Master for the power of what he seemed to have done. And they were disbelieving of that power.

The man knew that he would never be accepted by the people. "Please take me with you," he said to the Master. "Please take me with you. I am not welcome here." All those in our boats who heard this drew back. One of us said aloud, "I am not riding back with him. He will kill us when we are in the middle of the sea." Some said, "He will make us unclean."

The Master looked at us in the boat. He turned back to the man with sadness. "You must stay here. These are your people. You must be the one to tell them all that *Abba* has done for you."

The man began to weep again. "You are going to leave me alone again? You came all this way and touched me and saved me, and now you are going to leave me? I have no family or friends. No one will ever touch me. Please let me come with you." The Master walked back to the boats and gazed at us for a long time. Some of us drew back in shame, all in fear, and some in anger and resentment. "How can he ask us to take this man into our boat? He is unclean. A gentile sinner. Why does he care for him more than he cares for us? What has this man done to deserve this? What

that. Jairus was one of those who believed that the LORD would rescue the people from the boot of the Romans when all Jews observed all of Torah for one full day. Jairus was one of those who believed that the people of God must remain pure and separate from the rest of humanity. The Master was always touching the unclean and then spreading the impurity around. The Master was always sharing table with sinners. The Master claimed the power to forgive independent of the temple, forgiving without even requiring the sinner to purify him or herself according to Torah. The Master's power of healing and the power of his words to pierce the heart were so great and undeniable that Jairus said that he must have a demon. Jairus felt that these gifts gave the Master that much more power to lead people down the wrong path.

But there Jairus was, waiting for the Master, standing with the unclean.

The Master stood face to face with Jairus, waiting. All he said to Jairus was, "Peace be with you, brother." The people around the Master were pulling at his cloak and calling for his mercy. But the Master stood silently before the elder. Jairus finally spoke. "I know, Teacher, that I have not been supportive . . . or even respectful of you. I know that I have condemned you to the people, and told them to stay away from you and your followers, and refused to share a meal with you. I know that I have kept you from preaching anymore in the gathering."

The Master still stood silently, gazing into Jairus's face intently, giving him the time to make his own words.

"If I were not desperate, I would not be here. I know that I do not deserve your mercy." And then Jairus began to weep. The Master put his arm around the elder's shoulder and led him through the crowd to a drying stand for fish. Those of us with him surrounded the two of them, giving them some space to talk. The Master raised his hand and looked out at the crowd. They quieted!

"What is it, brother?" asked the Master. "What do you need from me? Do not be afraid to ask."

"Teacher, it is my little daughter. She is ill, on the brink of death. She cannot keep any food or even water down. It has been so for many days. She is so weak she cannot even roll over on her pallet. The doctors can do nothing. Her mother is beside herself. She insisted that I come find you. When I refused, when I said that you would not come after the way I had treated you, when I said that you had a demon, my wife berated me that I loved Torah and my own righteousness more than I love my daughter.

The Master turned to him. "Peace, brother. This woman is as much our daughter as your own daughter is. I will come in good time. It will not be too late. It is this daughter's time now. Your daughter's time is about to come. Do not fear, but only believe."

The Master turned back to the trembling, fearful woman. Jairus screamed out a loud, guttural groan. "Cursed be you! You are of the devil! You purposely delay with this whore so my daughter will die. Do you not know who is deserving and who is not?" And he kicked the cowering woman as she had been kicked many times before.

The Master turned toward Jairus, took a step and stood face to face to him. "Jairus, you will never kick anyone again. Do you hear me? Never again. If you feel the need again to degrade some poor outcast with a kick, then you will kick me instead. I ask you again. Do you hear me?"

Jairus' face turned deep red, and his eyes filled with tears. I could not tell if it was from shame or anger.

The Master turned back to the woman. "Daughter, why did you touch me?"

"I am sorry. Please forgive me, Master. I thought that if I just touched the hem of your robe, that your healing angel would enter me and heal me. I have been waiting here, trying not to be ordered away just for the chance that you would walk by."

"Why did you not call out to me like the others do, asking me to heal you?"

"Why would you? I am a sinner. I am unclean. I have been bleeding for a dozen years. The leader is right. I am cursed by God."

"Daughter, no one is cursed by God. Only men curse. Then they claim God's sanction. Have you no family to care for you?"

"None, Master. They have pushed me out."

"How long have you been abandoned by your family?"

"Since my father divorced my mother, since he charged that she had been with another man and publicly shamed her."

"Who was the other man?"

"I never knew him."

"And your father and his family?

"They will not see me."

"Did something start your bleeding?"

"I was pregnant. While I was pregnant and hungry, only a few weeks from my time, I went into a village to beg for food. A man called me a

"Come with me now, daughter."

The woman followed him. As he approached Jairus, a servant from Jairus' house said resentfully, "Why trouble the teacher any further. Your daughter has died while he was touching that whore."

"Do not fear," said the Master to Jairus. "Trust *Abba*. Lead me to your house."

He turned to the crowd. "I am asking you, out of respect for a child who is in need, wait for me here. Do not follow me up that hill." Then he turned to me. "Simon, only you, James and John will come with me. I do not want to frighten his daughter."

Then he took the hand of the woman. "And you, daughter. Come with us."

Jairus spoke up, as if from a trance. "My wife will not let her come into my house. She will make everyone unclean."

"Jairus. Jairus, please look at me. If your daughter is dead as your servant says, then your house is already unclean. But your child is not dead, only sleeping. And this new child of mine . . . she is no longer dead, but awake again after a long sleep forced upon her by the mercilessness of men. And she was never unclean in the eyes of *Abba*. Only *Abba*'s eyes count."

The healed woman's eyes grew wide.

As we walked up the hill away from the village and the sea, we could hear the sound of loud weeping and wailing. As we came closer to the leader's house, we saw a commotion. Jairus' wife was covering her face and arms in dirt, and tearing at her face with her fingernails. Young women around her, probably servants, were trying to subdue her.

The wife looked up and saw the Master. "It took you so long to come!?" To Jairus she said, "It took you so long to bring him!? And you see yourself as so important. You cannot bring a charlatan to the bedside of your only daughter until after she has died."

The Master said again. "Daughter, your daughter is not dead but only sleeping." The male servants who were with Jairus laughed derisively. "This man is a fool," one said.

The Master took Jairus, his wife, the woman who had been bleeding, and us into the house. As he entered, he said as always, "*Abba*'s peace be upon this house."

We walked to the daughter's bedroom. Jairus led the way.

The little girl lay unmoving on a pallet in the far corner. She was pallid and thin. Her eyes were closed. She did not appear to be breathing.

"I admit . . . . that I . . . felt that my family and I somehow deserved mercy, that we were due the LORD's mercy more than others, because of the way that I have tried to obey Torah. That the LORD somehow owed that to me as a matter of his justice and righteousness. Somehow I thought that my daughter deserved his mercy because of my righteousness. But then I saw how merciful you were to that woman. How you delayed coming to my house to save my daughter to save that sinner. At first I was angry with you. How can you have power from the LORD, as opposed to from Satan, if you were touching and healing such an unclean woman? But you were so kind. And you had the power to heal both of them, my daughter and that woman. And that woman was so sweet, her song was so sweet and heart rending, and she was so kind to my daughter. Surely such mercy must come from the LORD. I had never allowed myself to be around such a sinner before. It's as if I am seeing now where I did not before. Before today . . . I thought that those who deserved mercy received it from the LORD, and those who did not did not receive it. But I saw you heal the woman and then my daughter . . . So many children die. So many women are cast out. Why do some receive mercy and so many do not? When is the LORD merciful?"

"When the time comes," said the Master.

"When what time comes?"

"When the time comes that *Abba*'s mercy is born in all his children."

"So it is entirely up to us?"

"No. But we must live as if it is."

"Then how do we decide who receives the LORD's mercy from our hands. Who can be due such mercy?"

"No one," said the Master. "And so . . . everyone."